Contents

    List of illustrations   7
    Acknowledgments   9
    Map of Crete   10
1 Culture and History   13
2 The Mysterious Minoans   33
3 Heraklion and Knossos   39
4 The North-East Coast   48
5 Aghios Nikolaos   55
6 Around Aghios Nikolaos   61
7 The South Coast   86
8 Rethymnon   94
9 Chania   104
10 Exploring Western Crete   112
11 Food and Shopping   119
12 Sports and Activities   125
    Index   133

List of Illustrations

between pages 64 and 81

1 Fishermen in the harbour at Heraklion
2 Shopping in one of Heraklion's busy side streets
3 Cretan dress; traditional and more modern styles
4 Cretan seascape near Heraklion
5 Knossos: one of the site's giant storage jars
6 The 'Court Ladies' fresco, from Knossos
7 Murals in the Throne Room, Knossos
8 & 9 The 'Snake Goddess' statuette, and the Bull's Head, both from Knossos
10 The ruins at Malia
11 Tiny white villages nestling below huge mountains, near Gouria
12 Mount Idi and the Idi range, south-west of Heraklion
13 The monastery at Arkadi
14 The inner harbour at Aghios Nikolaos
15 Sponge fisherman at Aghios Nikolaos
16 Kritsa, one of the most beautiful and unspoiled villages in Crete
17 The Church of Panaghia Kera, near Kritsa, which dates from the thirteenth century
18 A country woman riding her donkey just outside Kritsa
19 The village of Elounda, near Aghios Nikolaos
20 A fisherman mending his nets beside the beach at Ierapetra
21 Europe's only palm-fringed beach, at Vai, near Sitia
22 Souvenirs with a difference: a Cretan shop-front
23 The remains of Aghia Triada, near Phaestos
24 The Gorge of Samaria, in south-west Crete

Acknowledgments

My thanks are due to the National Tourist Organization of Greece, both in Athens and London, for its help and hospitality while I was researching parts of this book. In particular, I am grateful to the Director of the Greek Tourist Office in London, Peter Analytis, and to his former deputy Miss Cleo Angelopoulou (now based in Athens) for their assistance and encouragement. Vital information and facilities were also provided by British Airways, Owners' Services Ltd and Chandris Hotels, and by the following individuals: Robin Bean, Jenny Crayford, Richard Davies, Peter Drew, David Dougall, Kaye Economou, George Harris, Basil Iatrides, Basil Mantzos, Marion Mead, Mario Modiano, Sia Moraitou, Kelvin Moyses, Eleni Nakou, Katie Pirounakis, Peter Roberts, Ron Scobling, Maggie Southam, Polly Spentza and Michael Xenakis. And finally my thanks must go to Johanne Grimshaw, who not only typed the manuscript but ensured that I stuck to my writing schedule.

The author and publisher would like to thank the following people for providing photographs: J. Allan Cash Ltd: 1, 3, 4, 7, 11, 12, 14, 23. Douglas Dickins: 5, 15. Droba-Noble Photography: 22. Feature-Pix: 13, 19. Robert Harding Picture Library: 8, 9, 16. Ronald Sheridan's Photo-Library: 6. The author's own collection: 17, 18, 20, 24.

The map of Crete on p. 10 was drawn by Lt.-Col. W. F. N. Watson.

1 Culture and History

The visitor to Crete, whether he is arriving by sea or by air, sees the mountains first. Three great ranges dominate, indeed almost make up, this largest of the Greek islands, one hundred and sixty miles long, giving it an atmosphere and scenery quite unlike those of the gentle Cyclades islands to the north. The mountains – the Dikti Range in the east, the central Idi Mountains, and the huge Lefka Ori, or White Mountains, in the west – where the snow lingers on until late in May when the beaches far below are simmering in the hot summer sunshine, give Crete a hard, rugged appearance. It does not look like a holiday island.

So why has Crete become Greece's fastest-growing holiday destination, with hundreds of thousands of visitors pouring in from all over Europe every year?

The answer, I think, is that Crete is an island with which it is all too easy to fall in love. It is beautiful, romantic, dramatic, a high and often mysterious island with scenery very like that of the Scottish Highlands yet the advantage of vast beaches, modern hotels, the long hours of sunshine which befit Europe's most southerly point, and an unspoilt atmosphere that is perhaps more Greek than anywhere in the rest of Greece.

Historical links with mainland Greece and the other islands, coupled with the fact that the mountains often end dramatically in soaring cliffs and deep gorges on the south coast, have meant that Crete's main towns are on the north coast.

From the west they are Chania, the island's former capital and still described by some authorities, quite incorrectly, as the capital of Crete; Rethymnon; the present capital and main port of Heraklion; and, in the east, the rapidly-growing resort of Aghios Nikolaos. Although there are ferry services from the mainland to both Chania and Aghios Nikolaos, and Chania has an airport, most visitors arrive at Heraklion. It is an ugly, sprawling, yet strangely attractive city which is, surprisingly, the fifth largest city in Greece. Relays of sleek car ferries make the overnight run between Heraklion and the mainland port of Piraeus, one hundred and sixty miles to the north, on a daily basis, while the airport has regular links with Athens as well as being journey's end for charter flights from all over Europe. Indeed, one of the principal disadvantages of holidaying in Crete is that Heraklion Airport is totally incapable of dealing with the volume of traffic which it is now attracting, and the visitor might be introduced to Greek inefficiency and occasionally dubious manners in the long queues which form at the immigration desks and in the luggage hall of Heraklion Airport, which it can take well over an hour to clear.

Conversely, it is here that one gets one's first taste of Crete too. For, even on some charter flights, one's fellow passengers are likely to include a fair smattering of islanders returning home – the men unshaven, baggy-trousered, probably pullovered despite the heat, and often impressively moustached; the women in black peasant clothes, or perhaps the latest fashions (depending partly upon their social status, but more often on age); the children excited and noisy; and all of them carrying inordinate amounts of hand baggage which more often than not is stored in rapidly disintegrating brown paper parcels.

The men of Crete have a motto, one they will relate to the visitor on every possible occasion. It is: 'Crete's weather is like its people – usually nice but able to get rough very quickly.' Somehow that sums up both Crete and the Cretans. For just as Crete is a rugged, individualistic island, so the Cretans have a rugged individuality that can be compared with the characteristics of Yorkshiremen, or Texans in the United States. They are part of a nation with everything in the way of national pride and character that this involves, and yet they manage to retain their individuality; one is always aware that if they ever had to choose between Greece and Crete it would be Crete every time. They fought a long and savage guerilla war against their Turkish masters from the Middle Ages right up to comparatively recent times, and when the Germans occupied the island during the Second World War they were never able to exercise full control over the Cretans, who fought all over the vastness of Crete's three great mountain ranges where a handful of men with local knowledge could hold an army at bay.

The shape of the Mediterranean means that Crete, besides being the largest island in the eastern Mediterranean (with the exception of Cyprus), is on the same latitude as north-west Africa. Thus it is the most southerly point in Europe, and on the coastal plains it is blessed with warm sunny weather for most of the year. These late autumns and early springs contrast strangely with the snow which lingers so late up in the hills.

The Greeks wax lyrical about the place. One official tourist office description of the island boasts: 'The trip to Crete is actually a pilgrimage. Every town, every village of the *megalonissos* (big island) has something to show, something special to tell. Wherever in Crete, the visitor will feel the warmth of home and the one to know Crete will never forget it. A trip to this island is a spiritual relax (*sic*) and the storage of cherished memories.'

A trifle effusive perhaps, yet impossible to contradict. Crete is an island with the unique ability to make the visitor feel somehow as though he belongs.

Homer, the classical Greek poet whose criticisms and comments about his own country comprise perhaps the first ever travel guides, thought the same. He described Crete as 'fair and fertile', and such praise from Homer was hard to come by (he dismissed the Ionian island of Ithaca, for instance, as 'a precipitous isle, unfit for horses . . . or for goats.') But 'fair and fertile' is certainly an assessment of Crete which remains true to this day. Fair it certainly is, with scenery ranging from the palm-fringed beach at Vai in the far east of the island, to the soaring cliffs and the rocky paths of the Gorge of Samaria – Europe's longest and deepest gorge – in the West, and from the dramatic ruins of Knossos in the north to the sandy beaches of the pretty little fishing port of Ierapetra in the south. And, despite its barren appearance, Crete is a surprisingly fertile island too. There are extensive vineyards on the coast, while higher in the mountains, where there is often an unexpectedly large area of cultivated land, the villages grow enormous quantities of vegetables and other market garden produce. Citrus fruits abound, of course, and there are olive trees everywhere – nets spread beneath them so that not a single olive shall go to waste. They even grow bananas in Crete. Indeed, were it not for the visitors, Crete would be very close to self-sufficiency – for the island produces its own wine, there is sufficient meat, and there are always plenty of fish in the Aegean Sea to the north or the Libyan Sea to the south. The present population is about half a million, but experts suggest that a six-fold increase would not strain its resources.

Most of the holiday development on the island has been along the north coast – particularly on the beach between Heraklion and Aghios Nikolaos where a very good modern road has replaced the tortuous mountain tracks which linked the two cities less than a decade ago. New resorts have sprung up around hotel developments at places like Malia and Gournes. They have the advantage of fine beaches, but might not be everyone's choice for a Cretan holiday because in summer the north coast often has a persistent north wind blowing off the Aegean and called the *meltemia*. The *meltemia* may serve to cool the scorching summer heat, but it can also whip the sand uncomfortably off the beaches. And much of the development is 'touristy' too – with rather un-Greek *tavernas*, serving chips with everything, and cheap souvenir shops specializing in 'I went to Crete' tee-shirts, fake Cretan vases, and over-priced sponges.

Aghios Nikolaos, which has grown from a tiny fishing village into a major tourist resort within the space of ten years, has also suffered some despoilation. But 'Ag. Nik.', as some visitors will insist upon calling it, has somehow managed to retain its attraction despite this. It owes its popularity, no doubt, to television exposure in Britain during the series *The Lotus Eaters* and *Who Pays the Ferryman?*, but it is also a resort which many people visit on the recommendation of their friends, and the main British inclusive tour operators all feature Aghios Nikolaos. At the western end of the island, Chania and Rethymnon are both attracting an increasing holiday trade, whilst many younger people are heading for the remote and completely unspoilt south coast villages which were 'discovered' by the hippies, who found that they could live there very cheaply and that there was no-one to object if they chose to go bathing in the nude. Nude bathing is, incidentally, illegal in Greece and the police in Crete are quicker than most to clamp down on anyone giving offence to the locals – but what the visitor chooses to do on a totally secluded beach is unlikely to produce any serious repercussions.

Farming excepted, Crete has almost no industry. Most of Crete's inhabitants live and work in villages, but tourism is starting to play an increasingly important role in the life of the island and new developments are taking place all the time. Some of the new hotels are particularly impressive, although all but a handful of them tend to be run with the cheerful inefficiency that one associates with the eastern Mediterranean.

But then visitors to Crete are unlikely to complain – for it is the island's ambience, and its antiquities, that they have come to savour. The long history of Crete is expressed in its ancient ruins: the Minoan palaces of Knossos and Phaistos; the villas in the classical and Roman cities of Gortyn and Lato; the Byzantine churches, and the Venetian castles.

The history of Crete is as turbulent as its geography; sometimes mysterious, often violent, occasionally romantic. And, as so often seems to be the case with Greek history, fact and fiction seem to become inextricably intermingled.

The archaeologists say that the first inhabitants of Crete arrived 8,000 years ago, probably from Anatolia. They were a Neolithic people, and their stone artefacts and weapons have been found on the island along with some female figures which are thought to indicate a mother goddess cult – an interesting foretaste of the Minoan culture which was to follow.

Greek legend tells a far more complicated story, and places Crete at the centre of many of the fascinating and heroic tales of the gods and goddesses, semi-mortals and mortals, who created and populated this land and who some Greeks believe hold sway over the world even to this day.

Just as the stories of Robin Hood have become a part of English folklore, so the old stories of the Creation, the battles between the gods on Mount Olympus, the heroic deeds of Heracles (the Romans called him Hercules) and the Trojan War were passed on from mouth to mouth and from generation to generation, and even partly recorded in the ancient and only recently deciphered Linear-B script. This rich story of legend was known as the 'epic cycle' and it was much drawn upon by the blind poet Homer as well as by later poets and dramatists. By recording these epics in composite form, Homer was unwittingly presenting historians of the future with a picture of contemporary Greek values as well as beliefs. Furthermore, he was laying the foundations of the classicism from which the writers and artists of the Renaissance – among them Botticelli, Rubens and Shakespeare – were to draw inspiration. He was also providing a key to some of the great mysteries which archaeologists are still trying to unravel in the eastern Mediterranean. For example, everyone assumed that his tales of the bloodthirsty struggles between the Acheans of Greece and the Phrygians of Troy, between 1194 and 1184 BC, were part of a myth, until the German archeologist Schliemann, using Homer's tales as his guide, actually unearthed the foundations of Troy.

The deeds of each of the Olympian deities, the story of Jason and the Argonauts, the labours of Heracles, the history of the Trojan war, the separate Cretan and Theban myths, and the wanderings of Odysseus – all are told in the ancient legends. But besides forming the basis of the people's religious beliefs, and relating what was supposed to be the history of the Eastern Mediterranean world, the legends also served to explain some of the natural phenomena of the time and the area. The smoke and flames pouring from volcanic Mount Etna in Sicily, for example, was said to be due to the burial beneath the mountain of one of Zeus's enemies. A cave in the west of Crete, the Dictaean Cave, is where Rhea (sister of Uranus and wife of Cronus) is said to have hidden Zeus, as a child. Cronus swallowed all Rhea's children at birth so as not to be deposed by one of his own sons, but she was determined to save Zeus and managed to hide him in the cave.

That there is such a thing as a Hellenic race at all is another point at which the historians and the storytellers diverge. Archaeologists say that the Hellenic people on the mainland of Greece were a northern, Aryan race, equipped with horses and wheeled vehicles, who moved into mainland Greece in about 2000 BC and fused with Mediterranean stock who had spread into the country a thousand years earlier and replaced the indigenous Neolithic people. The Mediterranean people had long enjoyed a civilization of their own centred upon the Cyclades islands. But what of the Minoan people of Crete? Was their civilization a natural extension of their Neolithic beginnings, a culture which had developed naturally in the mountainous vastness of their highland home? Or were they influenced by trade links with the highly civilized Egyptians close by? Archaeologists and historians are still arguing about the answers to those questions.

Be that as it may, the Aegean Sea was certainly a busy thoroughfare during this period, and extensive trade links had been formed between the peoples bordering its edges. The Aegean is largely cut off from the rest of the Mediterranean; it is in effect an island-studded lake, bounded to the north and west by the Greek mainland, to the east by Turkey, and to the south by Crete. It is known that the Cretans had built up an extensive trading community in these waters, where the fact that a sailor was seldom out of sight of land made sea travel comparatively simple. Largely as a result of these trading opportunities the Cretans had become relatively prosperous and, more importantly, they were apparently without enemies. The Cretans built extensive and unfortified settlements at places like Knossos, near the present capital of the island, Heraklion, and at Phaistos in the south. Close by, in the Cyclades, the islanders turned to mining, and traded in copper and gems. Man had ventured to Asia and Africa to find tin with which copper must be combined to make bronze.

The Minoan civilization at Knossos is named after the legendary King Minos of Crete, whose horrific bull-headed son, the Minotaur, was reputed to be kept in a labyrinth of passages. The Athenian prince Theseus was able to find his way and kill the Minotaur only by using a reel of thread, in order to be able to retrace his steps. When the archaeologist Sir Arthur Evans excavated Knossos in 1900 the ruins that he found were so extensive that he thought at first he had discovered the legendary labyrinth, and that – as in the case of Troy – another of the old stories had come true. In fact he was in the luxurious palace of Knossos, built in a style centuries ahead of its time. Lightwells let in the sunshine, there were efficient washing and toilet facilities and the cellars were found to be stuffed with jars of food and wine.

Those were the days of wine and roses in the Aegean. Painting, sculpture, sport – such were the pastimes of a people who had both the leisure and the wealth to indulge themselves. That, at least, is the theory propounded by Sir Arthur Evans – and still the one adhered to by most archaeologists. But the German archaeologist, Professor Hans Georg Wunderlich, has put forward an alternative proposition. He points to some extraordinary omissions on the part of the builders of Knossos – such as the lack of kitchens or stables among the hundreds of rooms, and the fact that the royal apartments are at a very low, dimly lit level. Wunderlich also notes that the Linear-B texts, translated after Evans's death, were in an Ancient Greek dialect, which places a big question mark after the Evans hypothesis that the Minoan culture was essentially pre-Greek. In his book, *The Secret of Crete*, Wunderlich comes out in support of an earlier German critic of Sir Arthur Evans, the philosopher Oswald Spengler, who in the 1930s argued that the 'absence of any protecting wall around ancient Cretan palaces and country estates, the pictures of bulls so reminiscent of the ancient Minotaur legend and that peculiar king's throne in the Palace of Knossos, which in his view would be more suitable "for a votive image or a priest's mummy"' prompted him to ask: 'Were the "palaces" of Knossos and Phaistos temples of the dead, sanctuaries of a powerful cult of the hereafter?' The question, Wunderlich said, seems worthy of serious consideration. He goes on to argue a strong Egyptian influence in Minoan Crete, and offers evidence that the palaces of Crete were indeed mausoleums to early cult figures, carrying on the heroic culture of the Ancient Greeks.

Whatever the answer to this fascinating archaeological riddle, nature was to intervene dramatically in the Aegean.

It is still not known quite what happened, or when. Perhaps this Aegean civilization was the mysterious Atlantis, and doubtless if it had been allowed to continue the history of the entire area, and perhaps of the world, would have been very different. But, some time around 1500 BC, a cataclysmic earthquake or volcanic eruption shattered the area. The clues are few and far between, but the Greek legend of Deucalion and the flood, the biblical story of the parting of the Red Sea, modern radio-carbon dating and, in the middle of the Aegean, the visual evidence of the extraordinary sunken crater and the islets, one of them still smoking, that make up Santorini, all point to a volcanic eruption of unimaginable proportions. Indeed, Santorini still reminds one irresistibly of what it in fact is: an enormous volcanic crater peeping above the waves.

Santorini is estimated to have exploded with a force three times greater than Krakatoa's, whose eruption in 1883 killed some 36,000 people in Java and Sumatra with tidal waves, and was heard 2,000 miles away. Santorini, then known as Thira, all but disappeared; the north coast of Crete, every Aegean island, and most ports on mainland Greece must have been devastated. Few vessels in the Mediterranean could have remained afloat, and the loss of lives must have been enormous. The glorious Minoan culture on Crete, which – assuming it existed – had no enemies but nature, disappeared beneath the waves or else was buried under a hundred and thirty feet of volcanic ash.

At this point, Crete disappears from the mainstream of Greek history. The cities or palaces of Knossos and Phaistos had been too well built on high ground to have been damaged by the tidal waves caused by the explosion of Santorini, but the distribution of volcanic ash would have been sufficient effectively to put an end to any agriculture on the island for many years. Indeed, there is evidence to suggest that the Cretans saw the disaster coming, and fled from the island before the actual eruption – a fact which would account for the absence of any human remains in excavations at the island's ancient sites. In his book, *The End of Atlantis*, Professor J. V. Luce suggests that the merchants and farmers of Keftia, the name by which the ancient Egyptians knew Crete, suffered too greatly to rebuild what had been the Minoan civilization. They gathered together what little they could salvage and set sail to find new homes. They would have followed the old sea routes with which their captains and sailors were familiar: westwards to southern Italy and Sicily, northwards to the Cyclades and Attica, eastwards to Rhodes, Cyprus and the Levant, and southwards to Egypt. But they sailed no longer as masters of the sea and chief traders of the eastern Mediterranean. They were now exporting themselves, not their goods. Says Professor Luce: 'A remnant of this Minoan dispersion may have settled as far away as Tunisia, where a tribe of "Atlantes" was known in the classical period. A remnant certainly went eastwards and settled in the coastal strip of southern Palestine, and were later known as Philistines. The prophet Amos refers to this migration and, interestingly enough, links the event with a description of vulcanism and inundation.'

Behind them, the Minoans left a legend which was to become one of the world's great mysteries: the legend of Atlantis. Were the civilizations of the Cyclades or Crete the basis of the story of the 'lost continent' of Atlantis? Was Santorini, the island which all but disappeared in that cataclysmic explosion, itself Atlantis? Archaeologists seem to be coming round to the point of view that Atlantis was on Santorini, although the evidence is fragmented. One of the principal arguments against it is that Plato placed Atlantis firmly out in the Atlantic, a location given credence by the fact that Schliemann used similar legendary evidence to find Troy. Plato, in fact, described Atlantis as 'an island situated in front of the Straits which are by you called the pillars of Heracles [Gibraltar]', and said that the island was 'larger than Libya and Asia put together'. The island of Atlantis was 'pre-eminent in courage and military skill, and was the leader of the Hellenes. But . . . there occurred violent earthquakes and floods; and in a single day and night of misfortune . . . Atlantis . . . disappeared in the depths of the sea.'

This story has encouraged archaeologists to hunt for the lost continent all over the Atlantic Ocean and even beyond. There have been theories that Atlantis was Morocco, while an occult suggested that it was in Nigeria. One explorer claims to have seen the walls of its citadel on a submarine reef near Heligoland. Mexico, Peru, the islands of the Caribbean, and even Ceylon, have been identified as Atlantis.

But given Plato's skimpy knowledge of the world as it then existed, and the fact that he was relating a story which had never been written down, but which had been passed on through the centuries, opinion now prefers the theory that Atlantis was indeed the Minoan empire based on Crete and Santorini.

As the Minoans dispersed around the Mediterranean, mainland Greece stepped into the forefront of Greek history. The Mycenaeans, led by King Agamemnon, were warlike people who had united mainland Greece and, although they had inherited some aspects of Minoan culture such as writing, they were more interested in conquest. They sent slave traders to Syria, Cyprus and the coastline of Asia Minor. They formed a fleet of 1,200 ships to attack Troy – the expedition that was to be the basis of the last, and perhaps the greatest, of the Greek legends. And their rule foundered only when a more barbarous people from the north, the Dorians, who were armed with iron swords, swept down from what are now Bulgaria and Yugoslavia to sack the Mycenaean cities. The Mycenaeans withdrew to the Greek islands.

But the coming of the Iron Age did more than revolutionize warfare; it revolutionized farming too. The mainland city states, like Sparta and Corinth, sprang up – the forerunners of modern communities with an economy based partly on commerce and partly upon the surrounding farmlands. From these city states adventurers once again set sail to explore and colonize the Aegean world and beyond. The mainland and island races merged once again and the neighbouring Italians coined a word for these emergent people from the east: Greeks.

Intellectually, this was a period of great development in the eastern Mediterranean. Religion, based upon the worship of the gods on Mount Olympus, was widespread, and religious centres like Delphi attracted a considerable following. Writing returned to the country, although the new Greek alphabet was Phoenician, and philosophy, poetry and science all reappeared. In Athens, a city which was well placed geographically and was surrounded by fertile land, democracy was born through the creation of a governing council for the city drawn from all classes, and the establishment of courts and the jury system.

Once again, the Greeks were hundreds of years ahead of their time. And once again, mankind was to suffer a setback. This time the problems were the development in the Middle East of a powerful military rival, Persia. The Persians, whose empire already stretched from India to Asia Minor, cast covetous eyes upon Greece, and there followed one hundred years of military struggle when Darius (and, after him, Xerxes) both sent massive military expeditions to try to capture Greece. They failed, but democracy suffered in that Athens emerged from the war all powerful and, instead of championing Greek freedom, became the overlord of a country that once more centred itself on the Aegean. Art and culture flourished at this time, with the bas-relief now known as the Elgin Marbles (which decorated the Parthenon and are now in the British Museum) being executed during this period, the dramas of Sophocles and Euripides becoming popular, and the schools of philosophy led by Socrates, Plato and Aristotle, all flourishing. But war between Athens and neighbouring Sparta again caused a setback, and it was left to a Macedonian prince, Alexander the Great, to unite the country with a war of conquest which he then turned into a crusade against Greece's old enemy, Persia.

Although the deeds of Alexander are of only peripheral interest to this book, they are extraordinary by any standards. He was just twenty when he ascended to the throne of Greece, upon the assassination of his father. The Greeks dismissed him as 'merely a crazy boy' and launched a series of revolts against him. He crushed them with ease, collected together an army of 35,000 men, crossed the Hellespont, freed Troy from the Persians, crushed the Persian army, then resolved to break Persian seapower by capturing every enemy port between Troy and Egypt. When the Persian king sued for peace, Alexander retorted: 'You must address me as Supreme Lord of all Asia. If you claim your kingdom, stand and fight for it.'

Small wonder that Alexander became the greatest Greek hero of them all. He captured Gaza, founded the Nile port of Alexandria, captured Libya, turned back to crush a new Persian challenge, then marched on unopposed through Babylon and the legendary Persian capitals of Suza, Persepolis and Ectabana, and on into India. He was still only in his mid-twenties. And he might have extended the new Greek empire all the way to China if disturbances in Persia had not compelled him to return to Babylon. He married a Persian princess, Roxana, but died, probably of malaria, in 323 BC; the empire rapidly fragmented because of the murder of the son Roxana bore him and his death-bed wish that his kingdom should go 'to the strongest'. Three Macedonian generals divided up his empire, and the divisions, rivalries and conquests which followed were to last until Greece became part of the Roman Empire.

The Romans were fascinated by Greek culture, appalled by the country's internal decay, and felt threatened by half-hearted Greek attempts to play at power politics in the Mediterranean vacuum. Rome finally decided to protect the Greeks from outside aggression and from themselves, and after two military victories over the Greeks in 196 BC Flamininus announced that Rome would henceforward be 'the protector' of Greece. The Greeks were forced to accept the inevitable as the Roman emperor Augustus imposed 'the Peace of Rome' all the way from Britain to Babylon.

It was at this time that Christ was born in Bethlehem, and it is worth recalling that as Greek was the common language of the eastern Mediterranean at this time, Jesus must have known and used Greek. But despite the faith that the Apostle Paul, a Hellenized Jew, was to bring to Asia Minor and to mainland Greece, it took three hundred years for Christianity to take firm root in the eastern Mediterranean. While Christians were still being martyred in Rome, Roman emperors like Hadrian were worshipping the pagan Greek gods. The religious breakthrough came when the Emperor Constantine was converted to Christianity and granted Christians religious freedom. To this day Constantine, who died in AD 337, is known to Greeks as the founding father of the Greek Orthodox religion which is common throughout Greece.

The city which Constantine had built seven years before his death on the site of old Byzantium, on the western shore of the Bosphorus dividing Europe and Asia, was to flourish as an oasis of culture throughout the dark ages of Europe. Named Constantinople after its founder, it sent missionaries and teachers out into the Balkans and Russia, to form literary and religious links which remain to this day. The Byzantines – as the people under Constantinople's sway were called – made mosaic pictures with bits of glass embedded in wet plaster, a classic art form of which good examples can still be found in Constantinople (now called Istanbul), Ravenna in Italy, and throughout the Aegean. Byzantine artists also practised fresco painting, the art from that was to spark the Italian Renaissance. Many Mediterranean churches boast fine fresco paintings, and there are some particularly striking examples to be found in Crete. Religious feelings were also expressed in small painted wooden panels called *icons*, the Greek word for 'images', which can also still be found in the eastern Mediterranean.

Crete, meanwhile, was beginning to emerge from the long years of isolation where it had remained a backwater of classical and Hellenistic culture – years during which the cities and coastal plains had sprung back to life but which were marred by inter-city warfare. The 'Peace of Rome' reached the island in 67 BC, when it was conquered by Metellus Creticus and designated the capital of the Roman province of Crete and Cyrenecia. The Cretans did not give up their island without a fight, and the Roman conquest was a bloody affair. But, once established, the Romans brought to Crete its first new cities since Minoan times – with Gortyn being built as the headquarters of the provincial governor. Roman villas also appeared on the island, notably at Gortyn and at Knossos.

The island continued to flourish in the early Byzantine years. But Constantinople was to be rent apart by power struggles and intrigues which were to make it an easy prey for its covetous neighbours – a factor which made it an enthusiastic host for the Crusades against the emergent Saracens in the east. Crete was an early casualty in this religious and military confrontation between east and west, and was quickly conquered by the Saracens who held it from AD 823 to 961. The Emperor Nikephoros Phokas freed the island in a savage campaign which culminated in his executing his prisoners and catapulting their heads into the Saracen stronghold of Heraklion – a calculated act of horrific cruelty which any Cretan will tell you was quite justified in that it brought about the expulsion of the invaders and the freedom of Crete.

But Constantinople was doomed, and with it its sphere of culture and influence. In 1204 the Venetians diverted the Fourth Crusade, originally aimed at the Holy Land, and hurled it against Constantinople. The city's gigantic and supposedly impregnable walls were breached and the city was sacked. During three days of pillaging, the work of 800 years was undone. Broken, Byzantium disintegrated into feudal states – and although there was a brief thirteenth-century revival of Byzantine influence, the old empire's vital trade routes had passed to the Venetians and the Genoese. The Genoese held Crete in the early part of the thirteenth century, then sold it to Venice in 1210. The Venetian occupation of Crete was to last more than four hundred years, until 1669.

Although they were merchants, the Venetians believed in guarding their business interest with an iron fist. They built a number of massive castles and walls to guard Crete's developing ports and harbours – at Heraklion, Chania, Rethymnon, Spinalonga, Ierapetra and Sitia. Trade flourished, including the sale of Cretan wine to Tudor England. And so too, perhaps surprisingly, did Cretan art – with this period being the golden age of Cretan fresco painting and icon painting.

Much of the rest of Greece had long since disappeared into the Turkish Empire – the Ottoman Empire, as it was to become known. Although they were not cruel masters, the Turks did treat the Greeks very much as a subjugated race – a fact which lies behind Graeco-Turkish animosity to this day. The one real benefit of the occupation was that the Turks allowed the Greeks religious freedom, so that the Orthodox Church survived more or less intact.

In 1669, the long arm of the Turks stretched out to Crete. Turkish forces captured the island from the Venetians, and Crete began yet another long occupation – this time of more than two hundred years. Crete no longer prospered, for the Turks traded little, and life on the island became harsh. Many of the islanders retreated into the hills and into themselves, creating a style of village existence and self-sufficiency which survives to this day. Occasionally they rose up against their Turkish masters – most notably in 1821 (when mainland Greece won its freedom and independence from the crumbling Ottoman Empire) 1828, and 1866. But these risings were always crushed, often savagely, and Crete remained a forgotten outpost of Europe.

The preoccupation of the nineteenth-century European great powers with maintaining a strategic balance in the Mediterranean was to delay the fulfilment of Cretan aspirations for several more years. In 1898 the Cretans finally threw out their Turkish masters – but the island was refused permission to unite with Greece because Greek politicians had spent the previous half-century indulging in some smart land-grabbing and power politics which had offended and worried Great Britain, France and Russia. Feelings over reunification ran so high on Crete that there was almost a civil war, and it became the task of the politician Eleutherios Venizelos to dabble in the murky waters of international diplomacy in search of a solution. Through a succession of Balkan alliances, he was finally able to persuade the great powers to recognize both Crete and the island of Samos as Greek territory, and in 1913 Crete was formally reunited with Greece.

But the island's troubles were far from over. The First World War loomed, and with it an internecine struggle between the new king, Constantine, and Venizelos. Constantine, brother-in-law of the Kaiser, favoured the Germans; Venizelos disagreed, was dismissed, and set up a rival government which split the country. Fortunately, Allied intervention forced the king to flee before the divisions became too marked, and Venizelos finished the war a hero. As a reward to him, the Versailles Peace Conference agreed upon the setting up of a Greek enclave on the Turkish coast at Smyrna, which Venizelos hoped would be a refuge for Greeks in the area. The idea was to prove disastrous. As a result of a national plebiscite King Constantine returned to Greece and decided to make up for past failures by launching a full-scale attack upon Turkey from the base at Smyrna. The Greek army suffered a shattering defeat, and the Turks recaptured Smyrna, and sacked and burned it. King Constantine abdicated, an army junta seized power in Athens, and Venizelos was again asked to pick up the pieces.

This, with Cretan help, he was able to do. Venizelos negotiated with the Turks an extraordinary exchange of populations – about 1,250,000 Greeks in Anatolia leaving to return to Greece, and 400,000 Turks leaving Greece. Many of the Greek refugees chose Crete as their new homeland, and settled on the outskirts of Heraklion and other main towns. Venizelos became Prime Minister of Greece, a post he held until he was ousted by another army coup. He died in exile in 1936.

The new leader of Greece was an army general called Ioannis Metaxas, a dictator who modelled himself on Mussolini. But he was a man of far greater mettle than the Italian fascist leader, and he carefully avoided aligning Greece with the other fascist powers. Greece remained neutral at the outbreak of the Second World War. In 1940 the Italians seized Albania, Greece's northern neighbour, but Metaxas still seemed unmoved, and even attended a party at the Italian legation in Athens. Early next day, 28 October, the Italian ambassador called unexpectedly at his home and Metaxas, wearing only a bathrobe, opened the door himself. The ambassador asked for formal permission for Italian troops to cross into Greece, a move which would have linked Greece inextricably with Germany and Italy.

Gently, General Metaxas shook his head. '*Ochi*' (No), he said, then shut the door in the ambassador's face. It was a moment that Greeks still love to recall, and 28 October is now a national festival known as Ochi Day.

When the inevitable fighting began, the highly regarded Italian army proved no match for the Greek forces, and was pushed back into the Albanian mountains. Only the intervention of powerful German forces saved the Italians from a humiliating defeat.

British and Commonwealth forces joined the Greeks in attempting to make a stand on Crete, in 1941, and the island was strongly garrisoned and given massive naval protection. But, in what is now seen as one of the decisive battles of the war, German bombers operating from freshly-captured airfields in the Peloponnese sank a number of British warships, and the Cretan land forces proved to be poorly commanded. When the German invasion forces landed, one British airborne division was virtually wiped out, and although the unprotected British, Greek and New Zealand troops fought bravely, they were overwhelmed. Cretan partisans helped many of the trapped and defeated troops to escape across the Libyan sea to North Africa, while others stayed behind to join the partisans in the guerilla war which continued in the mountains right up until 1945. Unable to defeat the guerillas, and stung by attacks on their occupying forces, the Germans responded by burning several Cretan villages and shooting hundreds of hostages – deeds which live on very strongly in Cretan memories.

The art of forgiveness is not a Cretan attribute – history has seen to that. And there is a difference between the sort of friendship which the Cretan will offer to a new acquaintance, and the loyalty – often quite literally 'unto death' – that he has for his family, fellow-villagers, and fellow Cretans. Like all Greeks, it will be many years before a Cretan offers you his heart. Apparently logical and philosophical, the people of Crete still put pride before reason; passions can run high, and anger is not far below the surface if a Greek feels that he, or his country, is being insulted.

This is something which the visitor should always remember. Take one of the rocky roads (the reason, no doubt, that car hire is so expensive in Crete; they must shorten the life of a vehicle by years) up into one of the countless mountain villages, and you will firstly be an object of curiosity and secondly, a stranger to be made welcome with all the traditional Cretan hospitality which is such a pleasant – if sometimes embarrassing – feature of the island.

But these are mountain people with mountain ways. Pick a fight with a villager, and you have picked a fight with the entire village. In the remoter parts of Crete, the Italian-style vendetta still exists; and the blood feud is something in which even the police might hesitate to interfere. Admittedly the holidaymaker's innocent glass of *ouzo* in the *taverna* is unlikely to arouse such passions – but western European youths chatting up the local girls is one thing that could. Unmarried girls in Greece, at least outside the large cities, are fiercely protected by fathers, brothers, uncles and cousins, and honour is, quite literally, a matter of life and death. So the amorous holidaymaker should avoid moonlight assignations, or any other kind of meeting which could be open to misinterpretation. Even a visit to a Greek girl's home, to meet her parents, can be dangerous; in Crete such a visit is usually taken as indicating a forthcoming engagement.

But if true Cretan anger is something to be avoided at all costs, it is important to remember that this anger bears no relation to the daily slanging matches the visitor will see between drivers in Heraklion's narrow streets, or between *taverna* waiters and their customers. It often seems impossible to ask for directions, or even ask the time, anywhere in Crete without attracting a crowd of people who will offer conflicting advice, shout, and wave their arms about. The reason is simple enough though: few Cretans are willing to admit that they do not know the answer to a question, so they say the first thing that comes into their heads. Someone else contradicts them . . . and the slanging match is on!

However, the basic characteristics of Cretans are friendliness and hospitality, wherever you wander on the island. Britons and Commonwealth citizens are particularly welcome, and may find themselves being regaled with tales of wartime brotherhood. And one feels that, below the surface, the Cretans are tired of their struggles, and the stormy history which has surrounded them. They are content to fish or farm a little, and sit for hours over their evening drinks arguing about nothing more worldly than the price of boat repairing materials or animal feed.

The Cretans will not expect you to know their history, understand their ways, or speak their language – although they will be delighted if you try. They are proud of the natural beauty of their island, and will recommend you to the spots which most tourists never find. One man, learning that I intended to walk the length of the Gorge of Samaria in western Crete, justly famed as the longest, deepest and most beautiful gorge in Europe, spent hours trying to persuade me to visit an 'even more beautiful' gorge on the south coast. He tried to explain where this gorge was, and eventually we got out a map. No such gorge was marked, but after a moment of baffled searching he was undismayed. Of course, it would not be marked, he reasoned. 'If it were, then it too would be crowded with tourists.'

That the islanders recognise their own pride and intransigence is apparent in their humour, which is occasionally earthy but usually unexpectedly sharp. The most arrogant Cretans of all, they will tell you, come from the high hills of Sfakia, and one of these mountain dwellers, dressed in the traditional sheepskin jacket, baggy trousers and high boots of his people, and strung with guns and knives, once found himself unexpectedly by the water's edge on the coast near Chania. He had never seen the sea so near before, and watched in amazement as two young Cretan boys laughed and splashed in the waves. Eventually the boys spotted him and, in the manner of small boys the world over, began to ridicule his appearance.

The Sfakian, so the story goes, became angry. He beckoned the boys over and glowered at them. 'It is not seemly,' he told them sternly, 'to laugh at a man from Sfakia. For we are the bravest and strongest men on all Crete. There is nothing a Sfakian cannot do.'

'Can you swim then?' they answered cheekily. 'Of course I can,' said the Sfakian angrily. 'A man from Sfakia can do anything.' And when they laughed again, he strode into the sea.

Weighed down by his weapons, and by the sodden sheepskin jacket, he rapidly sank, and the boys had to drag him ashore. There he took a moment or two to recover, then he glowered at the boys once more. 'You see,' he said, his pride undented, 'the sea, which can support a whole fleet of ships, cannot hold one man from Sfakia.' And he strode off back into the mountains.

He is not entirely a legendary figure, for you can still find men like him all over Crete. But, for the most part, the island and its people have adapted themselves to the needs of modern tourism. Hotels are graded by the government, and standards are fairly rigorous. Roads may vary from the excellent to the appalling, but directional road signs either bear place names in both the Greek and Roman alphabets or else are repeated in the Roman alphabet a few yards farther on, so you are unlikely to get lost. And the ubiquitous *taverna* means the meals are never a problem.

The very existence of *tavernas* means that self-catering holidays, in a rented flat or bungalow, are particularly attractive in Greece; you can breakfast in your holiday home, have a picnic lunch on the beach, and eat out almost every evening for little more than the cost of housekeeping at home. There has been a rapid growth in the availability of self-catering accommodation on Crete in recent years, but it is important to make the booking before you go. Once you have arrived in Crete it is often very hard to find such accommodation, particularly in the high season, and local landlords will push up the prices when they see you coming. By leaving it until you are actually in Crete, you also miss out on inclusive flights or other travel arrangements. Various British tour operators specialize in this kind of holiday.

The National Tourist Organization of Greece is also very helpful, and deals with individual inquiries. Its London offices are at 195 Regent Street, W.1 (Tel: 01–734 5997). In Greece, the tourist board is known as E.O.T., and besides its head office in Athens (2 Amerikis Street) it has an efficient branch office in Crete at 1 Xanthoudidou Street, in the centre of Heraklion.

Besides the more usual ways of helping holidaymakers, E.O.T. is responsible for the tourist police – a marvellous innovation which other tourism-conscious countries would do well to copy. The task of the tourist police is, quite simply, to help tourists, and to enable them to fulfil this none-too-onerous task they have all the powers of an ordinary policeman. You will find tourist police officers, identifiable by their badges, at all the main docks and airports on Crete, as well as in such resorts as Aghios Nikolaos, during the holiday season. You can't find a room for the night? You've lost your purse? Your child is sick? Just ask a policeman – or, rather, a tourist policeman.

It might sound unnecessary, but in a country where you have to be wearing a uniform before anyone will take any notice of what you say, the tourist police are essential – perhaps due to some sort of rule about it taking an official to catch an official.

One word about bus services on the island. These are superb, with a network of routes radiating out from Heraklion, and the fares are extraordinarily cheap. If you are not part of a package tour group, and have no chartered coach to whisk you around, then there is no need to depend upon expensive taxis – you can get almost anywhere by bus, and the services are very regular. The only difficulty concerns visitors who want to get up into the remoter mountain villages, for it has to be remembered that the bus services are run for the convenience of the islanders rather than the holidaymakers. So the bus link between Heraklion and a typical village might well consist of, say, a bus from the village in the morning, so that villagers can spend a day shopping in town, and a return service to the village in the evening. This means that the visitor may well have to spend the night in the village before being able to catch the bus back into town. Even that is no great problem, however. In most places the traveller can always find a room for the night in a private house for a purely nominal sum, and the room will be both comfortable and spotless. Like all Cretan traditions, the tradition of hospitality dies hard.

2 The Mysterious Minoans

Quite why the Minoans should be a mystery, is something of a mystery itself. After all, there is plenty of archaeological evidence as to who they were and what they did. And the Archaeological Museum in Heraklion, which is one of the most interesting and exciting in Greece, is largely given over to finds from the Minoan palaces on the island – complete with graphic friezes depicting their way of life, largely a result of interpretation of the work of Sir Arthur Evans, the man who excavated Knossos nearby. But who were the Minoans? And where did their culture spring from? Those vital questions are still unanswered.

As explained in Chapter 1, the first inhabitants of Crete were the indigenous Neolithic people who arrived in the island, probably from Anatolia, about 8,000 years ago, in 6000 BC. Like other Neolithic peoples, they lived in caves or on easily defended hill-tops. But in Crete their progress appears to have been far more rapid than elsewhere; they developed pottery both for domestic use and as an art form, in addition to the stone tools and weapons which they had previously used. As the years passed they learned to build small, rectangular stone houses, and their burial rites appear to have changed in a manner which suggests that they abandoned, at least partially, the cult of ancestor worship. Perhaps instead of their ancestors they worshipped some sort of fertility goddess, of which figurines – with a strong African influence – have been found.

Perhaps life on the fertile island of Crete was easier for these early people than that experienced by their relatives elsewhere in Europe. Certainly there is evidence that in about 2,500 BC they changed the siting of their villages, and instead of building them on the hill-tops they began to populate the areas around natural harbours. But whether this was a natural development or whether they were influenced by other immigrations – from mainland Greece, from Asia Minor, from Egypt, or from Libya – is not clear. What is clear is that in the years which followed, up until the eruption of Santorini around 1500 BC, the Minoans produced one of the world's most advanced civilizations, with remarkably strong trading links with the rest of the Aegean and a culture which was highly advanced even by today's standards.

Indeed, if Sir Arthur Evans is to be believed, life for some in Minoan Crete in the years up to 1500 BC was little short of idyllic. The illustrations in the Archaeological Museum in Heraklion depict beautiful bare-breasted girls, and youths whose idea of competitive sport was to leap over a bull's horns. The Minoans had no natural enemies, and their towns and palaces were undefended. Harsher, and much disputed, interpretations of the available evidence suggests a different story: the worship of goddesses who were depicted in the bare-breasted form of Minoan figurines, and horrific sacrificial rites which involved bulls.

Sir Arthur Evans has much to answer for, and he has left a clouded trail for modern enthusiasts to follow. But his story is a romantic one. A one-time journalist and adventurer turned amateur archaeologist, he became Keeper of the Ashmolean Museum in Oxford at the age of thirty-three. Like many late nineteenth-century liberals, he espoused the anti-Turkish cause at a time when the Ottoman empire was crumbling, and vast areas of the Near East were opening up to western influence, learning and inquiry after four centuries of being shut off behind a crescent curtain.

Evans was not the first archaeologist to show an interest in Crete. That distinction fell to the German, Heinrich Schliemann, the discoverer of Troy, who had wanted to dig at Knossos after the discovery, in 1878, of some store rooms containing pottery jars on a mound near Heraklion. But the Turks still controlled Crete then, and the island was largely closed to outsiders with digs being prohibited. In 1893 Evans went to Athens to study some of Schliemann's finds on Mycenaean sites, and at about the same time his sister alerted him to the possibilities of the site at Knossos. Evans managed to make a preliminary journey to Crete, and noted the signs of a pre-Mycenaean culture. And then, in 1898, with the expulsion of the Turks, he saw – and seized – his chance. He bought part of the site of Knossos, and returned to the island to begin what is still perhaps the best known archaeological dig of all time.

When work began, on March 23, 1900, Evans cannot have cut a very impressive figure. He was, says C. W. Ceram, in *The March of*

Archaeology, a 'small, dreadfully near-sighted man, who always carried a small cane in order to feel his way along.' But he had a head start on other archaeologists, and because he owned his own site he was safe from outside interference. And fortune was with him; within a week he had found the first clay tablets with Linear-B script on them. Within three weeks he had found 700 such tablets.

The finds continued to come thick and fast, and Evans poured all his energy and money into the excavation. His discoveries were stunning. For the spades of his workmen rapidly uncovered the maze of rooms and passageways which make up the Palace of Knossos. But Evans and his chief assistant, Duncan Mackenzie, found too, that the years had not been kind to the palace. The great columns and ceilings which the Minoans had erected lay in a jumble on the floors. Partly on a personal whim, but also to protect the diggings, Evans decided upon a policy of reconstruction. The throne-room was re-covered first, stone columns were erected in place of the original wooden ones, and the ceiling of the Grand Staircase was rebuilt. The work continued until the mid-1920s, when the introduction of reinforced concrete speeded up the work. In his book, *A Guide to the Minoan Palaces*, Stylianos Alexiou, director of the Archaeological Museum in Heraklion, writes: 'Completed replicas of the wall paintings and the painted reliefs were then set up at various spots in the palace. All these efforts disrupted the unity and character of the palace, since some areas remained in the state left by the fire of the final destruction, while others acquired the gloss and style of our own epoch because of the use of bright oil paints.' Evans himself published six volumes about his work, entitled *The Palace of Minos at Knossos*, describing his work, but this does not give as complete a picture of the site and the finds made there as present day scholars might wish for. Nevertheless it does, in the words of Stylianos Alexiou, 'constitute a magnificent attempt, penetrated by a creative imagination, to recapture the historical reality lying behind the Minoan antiquities.' By the time that Evans died in 1941, at the age of 90, Knossos had been rebuilt, largely in its present form. Purists might argue that it had also been rebuilt in Evans's image. In his will, however, Evans donated the site to Greece.

Work on the site continues to this day, and is carried out by members of the British School in Athens. But although the finds continue, the academic arguments grow more heated. As described in Chapter 1, Professor Hans Georg Wunderlich argues that the

Palace of Knossos was not at the heart of an advanced and urban civilization, but is a sort of pyramid which was the centrepiece of a death cult similar to that practised in nearby Egypt. He has even gone to great lengths to prove that the stone jars found in abundance at Knossos, and believed to have been used for storage, are in fact burial urns. Whilst agreeing that the Minoans eventually put this cult behind them, and moved ahead of their Mediterranean neighbours in the development of art and intellectual evolution, he argues: 'To see nothing but gaiety and playfulness in all that is to misunderstand their ancient religion.' Could Cretan 'bullfights', in which young men gave up their lives as part of a sacrificial orgy, be a more likely explanation of those murals – not to mention being a precursor of today's bullfighting tradition in Spain and Portugal? It would certainly help to explain the bull's horns which so symbolize the Palace of Knossos and which, along with the ubiquitous stone jars, are found around every corner on the site itself.

While Evans was excavating Knossos, another archaeologist, the Italian Federico Halbherr, was undertaking parallel work at Phaistos, on the southern side of the island. Although as imaginative as his British counterpart, and far more flamboyant, Halbherr did not indulge in the orgy of rebuilding which marks Knossos. For that reason Phaistos is today perhaps the more interesting site for the expert, although Knossos is still an exciting and emotive spot for the layman. And, strange to say, the Cretans themselves seem to have a softer spot for Evans – an unlikely outcome of the arrogant and highhanded way in which he delved through, and perhaps re-wrote, their history. The two men have one thing in common: between them they found the lost civilization which Evans christened the Minoan civilization, and which pushed back the borders of Cretan pre-history to its very beginnings.

No doubt time, and the advance of learning, will answer the remaining questions about the Minoans. We can dismiss the romantic story of King Minos, Theseus, and the thread with which he found his way back through the labyrinth after killing the Minotaur. Perhaps we can dismiss the pictures in the Archaeological Museum in Heraklion too – and affirm that life in Minoan Crete was not quite as easy as Sir Arthur Evans supposed. But we cannot dismiss the wealth of superb pottery, the artefacts, the paintings and the mosaics which he found. They are there for all to see – and their presence underlines just why it is so important that a visit to Knossos must be linked with a visit to the museum.

Roughly speaking, the Minoan period can be divided up into sections, starting with the Early Minoan period. This is the Neolithic age, with copper gradually replacing stone as the material used for tools and weapons, and jewellery and vases still showing a strong Anatolian and northern African influence. The round Tholos tombs mark this period. The population of Crete increased considerably at this time, and there are the first signs of village life.

The palaces, and possibly kings, or at least a ruling or religious privileged class, date from about 1950 BC to 1900 BC, and mark the beginning of the Middle Minoan period. This is when town life developed on the main sites, and individual villas were built on the island at places like Malia. The palaces, at Knossos, Malia, Phaistos, and Aghia Triada, reflect a shift in the economic and social activity of Crete from the east to the centre of the island. Evidence of town life is fuller. It is thought that at about this time burial was indeed in clay jars, or small *pithoi*, similar to the storage jars found at Knossos. Fine pottery work dates from this period too, with the introduction of the brilliant thin-walled polychrome vases known as Kamares Ware. Metal techniques developed, with jewellery being more finely worked with granulation and filigree decorations, and the swords and daggers of the period have medial ribs. There is also evidence of a great improvement in transport, and it has been suggested that wheeled transport was introduced to the island at the beginning of the Middle Minoan period. Life, at least in the palaces, was the life of an affluent society with great resources of wealth and excellent craftsmanship and artistry. The palaces provided comfort in daily life as well as elegance, with their wide courts and exquisitely decorated rooms. Writing was introduced, and there are examples of this to be seen on the seals and clay tablets of the time; the hieroglyphics eventually developing into what is now known as Linear-A script, thought to be the first form of writing which actually represented sounds. There is evidence of increasing foreign trade, particularly from discoveries of obviously imported products in storage jars.

In about 1700 BC Crete was struck by an earthquake and most of the Middle Minoan buildings were destroyed. But there is no break in the continuity of Minoan culture. The palaces and villas were rebuilt, and the period up until the eruption of Santorini was the Minoan 'golden age'. It is in this period that most of the Minoan buildings which can be seen today were constructed, and the palaces are marked by open-plan rooms, lightwells, plumbing and drainage – all introductions of the period. Fresco paintings were used for decoration. Huge storerooms were built in the palaces to ensure that the occupants were always adequately supplied with food and drink. New towns like Palaikestro, Zakro and Gournia were developed. Commerce flourished and so did contacts with the Greek mainland, the islands of the Aegean, and the coast of Asia Minor. Cretan trading colonies were established outside the island, and the use of Linear-A script was extended throughout Crete. The still undeciphered Linear-A script can be found on what appear to be extensive lists kept by storekeepers at this time. There are religious finds from sacred caves and sanctuaries of the period too. If Evans's interpretation of life on Minoan Crete is correct, then this surely is the period he is illustrating.

But some time around 1500 BC nature intervened in the form of the natural disaster previously mentioned. The Minoan civilization was all but wiped out, and refugees from Crete spread themselves over the Mediterranean and beyond. There was a brief resurgence of the Minoan civilization at Knossos, known as the Late Minoan period, and it is from this time that the Linear-B script dates. But the glory that was Crete was dead, and Knossos did not remain inhabited for more than about another fifty years. According to some archaeologists, the Minoans had already left – and both the writing of the period and greatly changed burial methods suggest that the people of Crete were by now Mycenaeans, probably from the mainland.

So the picture of the Minoans is a confused yet fascinating one. What is undisputed is that they were far ahead of their time in many aspects of their life, and that they set the stage for much of what was to follow in the eastern Mediterranean. They left behind in Crete much that is of interest to the modern visitor, who will undoubtedly agree that, whatever they were doing, they at least chose to do it in idyllic surroundings. And if they also left behind a mystery, it is one with plenty of clues. Part of the fascination of a holiday in Crete, however hazy your knowledge of archaeology and history, is to follow just a few of those clues in the museum at Knossos, at Phaistos, and on the other, lesser known, sites.

You will not find the answers in a week or a fortnight, but the search is well worthwhile.

3 Heraklion and Knossos

Like so many parts of Greece, Crete can be a disappointment at first, and this may be because almost every visitor to the island arrives either by sea or by air at Heraklion, the principal port of the island on the north coast. It is the island's capital too – if Crete can be described as having a capital – although the Greeks, always ready to argue about absolutely anything, still dispute this, and there are those who will tell you that Chania, to the west, is the true island capital. What is undisputed, however, is that Heraklion is Crete's administrative and business centre, which one might suppose makes it the *de facto* capital.

At first glance, Heraklion is not a pretty town. But don't be disappointed – it grows on you. And it is steeped in history.

It is a mediaeval city built by the Saracens in 824 AD and originally known as Candia because of the ditch which surrounded the city. It became the capital of Crete during the Byzantine period, and retained its importance during the Venetian occupation. Under Byzantine rule, it became a provincial centre for both commerce and the arts, especially painting and letters. It was in Heraklion – the name that it was officially given in 1822 – that El Greco received his initial training as a painter. The Venetians built a massive wall around the city, which was considered to be the strongest in the Mediterranean, and this wall today splits the city into two parts: the old city within the walls and the new city which has extended beyond them both to the east and the west. The port, which has also stretched beyond the walls, is of less importance in Greece only to Piraeus, the port of Athens, and Thessalonika.

Only about a quarter of the present city of Heraklion lies within the Venetian walls, but this is still the most important, and the most attractive, part. It contains the shopping centre, the street market, the principal churches, squares, hotels, public buildings and the older residential areas with their narrow streets and tightly packed houses. In the centre of the old town, in Plateia Venizelon, is the tiny structure which has become the city's most famous landmark: the Morosini Fountain, or Lion Fountain. This was built by Francesco Morosini in 1626–28, and incorporates some fourteenth-century lion carvings at its base. It has recently been restored to its full beauty, but it is still treated with casual indifference by the people of Heraklion who – if a policeman is not looking – will even treat it to the ultimate indignity of leaning their bicycles against it. Around it are the souvenir shops, the airline ticket offices and the inevitable *tavernas* to be found in any Greek city, and a series of Heraklion's principal streets lead off from the square.

Opposite the fountain is St Mark's Church, built by the Venetians in 1239, but extensively rebuilt and restored since then and now used as a cultural centre. Also reconstructed since the Second World War is the old Venetian Armoury, now used as the city hall. This stands in the north-east corner of the square, at the top of 25 August Street, the city's main commercial street which leads from the square down to the old harbour. The small harbour also dates from Venetian times, and although the modern car ferries use a far larger port, a few hundred yards to the east, this original harbour is still used for fishing boats and pleasure craft. It is guarded by an early sixteenth-century fort, Rocca al Mare, which is decorated with three sculpted winged lions of Venice. The fort has recently been restored, and contains twenty-six rooms. Surprisingly, it is quite a steep climb from the harbour back up to the Morosini Fountain, and the leg-weary may find it worthwhile to step through the Venetian Loggia, backing on to the Armoury in 25 August Street, where there are seats in a peaceful little park. Just beyond the Loggia, in a shaded square, stands the church of Aghios Titos. Originally built in Byzantine times it later became the cathedral of the Latin archbishop, and was to see service as a mosque before being destroyed by an earthquake in 1856 and being completely rebuilt. Today it is decorated in a tasteful shade of pale blue, and has an impressive modern altar screen of wood picked out with gold. It is a small copy of St Sophia's, in Istanbul.

But instead of climbing back up the hill to the Morosini Fountain, one can make the circuit of the old city of Heraklion by continuing from the old harbour along the sea front and past the impressively vaulted sixteenth-century Arsenals opposite the modern harbour. These used to be used as warehouses, but are now undergoing further restoration work. Here the road divides, and one can continue on to the car-ferry terminals or take the twisting road up on the right past the Atlantis Hotel (which is the best in Heraklion and has a fine restaurant and a good roof-top swimming-pool) to Plateia Eleutherias (Liberty Square) and the Archaeological Museum. Socially, Plateia Eleutherias is the centre of present day Heraklion. It is a huge square close to the city walls, and on the tree-filled central island the *tavernas* and bars which ring the square have erected metal-topped tables and chairs where the people of Heraklion gather to take the evening air. Traffic in the square is very heavy, with a bus terminal close by, tourist coaches and taxis joining the crush, and early evening shoppers thronging the streets, so Heraklion's 'happy hour' has all the appearance of being a most chaotic affair. Waiters dodge nimbly through the traffic, crossing the road to serve the customers on the central island, and swifts wheel and scream overhead before settling down for the night. Yet the central island, as well as the forecourts of the surrounding roadside *tavernas*, are extraordinarily relaxing places to be at this delightful hour of the day. After a day sightseeing or on the beach, it is time to sit down, take stock, and decide how to spend the evening which lies ahead. The Greeks themselves take great delight in this little ceremony, and it is a habit into which the visitor quickly falls.

From the square, the main shopping street, Leoforos Vas Konstandinou, leads back to the Morosini Fountain. Although there is a smattering of souvenir shops in this street, it also contains fine jewellery, clothes and shoe shops – with the latter offering particularly good bargains as detailed in the chapter later on shopping. There are government offices on the south side of the street, occupying a block of Turkish-style buildings. Another of the town's main shopping streets is Kalokairinou, which dates from Venetian times, and leads to a second bus terminal serving the southern part of the island. The town's lively food market is centrally situated in 1866 Street, a narrow, pedestrianized thoroughfare which is at its liveliest early in the day.

Another spot worth visiting is St Mina's Church, which is in fact two churches, one large and the other small. The first, built in 1735, contains some exceptional Byzantine icons, whilst the larger church is the cathedral of Crete and contains a set of six icons painted by the sixteenth-century master, Mikhailis Damaskinos, who is thought to have been one of El Greco's teachers. And one should not miss looking at at least one of the city's original gates, of which there were five. The best of these is the Kainouria, or New Gate, reached from Evans Street, which dates from the latter half of the sixteenth century and is dramatic in that it shows just how thick the great Venetian walls were: no less than 45 yards. The Chania Gate, built in about 1570 and now restored, is also worth seeing. St George's Gate, on the main road from Plateia Eleutherias to eastern Crete, no longer stands, but as the road winds down through the walls one should notice the old fountain which is still in the wall on the left-hand side of the road.

Just inside the Kainouria Gate, the road to the right leads to the Martinengo Bastion, which is the tomb of the author Nicos Kazantzakis, who died in Germany in 1957 and, because of his somewhat unorthodox ideas, was refused full burial rites. On the rough stone that covers his grave, an inscription from his work reads: 'I hope for nothing. I fear nothing. I am free.'

As has been stressed earlier, a visit to the Archaeological Museum should be combined with the short trip out to Knossos. Ideally, one should see Knossos first, then the museum, and then pay a return visit to Knossos. But if time is limited a visit to the museum should come first, for it does much to explain what one will see at Knossos.

The museum, an unimpressive building built to fulfil a specific purpose rather than to be admired, and also designed to withstand any future earthquakes in the area, is open in the mornings and afternoons, and closed for about two hours in the middle of the day. It is also open on Sunday mornings, but is closed on Monday afternoons. The collection of Minoan art and artefacts which it contains is, of course, unique, and the sheer beauty of many of the exhibits, coupled with a lively presentation, make a tour of the museum something which many visitors repeat time and again.

The twenty spacious galleries are so organized that a visitor to the museum can step through Cretan history as it was detailed earlier in this book. The first gallery, for example, is devoted to the Neolithic and prepalatial period, i.e. from about 6500 BC to 2000 BC, and contains Neolithic vessels, ritual objects, figurines, pottery from the burial caves, stone vases from the cemetery at Nokhnos, and finds from the Tholos tombs of Messera. The rapid development of the Minoan culture is quickly apparent from the next two galleries, for already one sees Kamares-style vases from Knossos and small earthenware plaques depicting Minoan house facades. A column from

Heraklion and Knossos 43

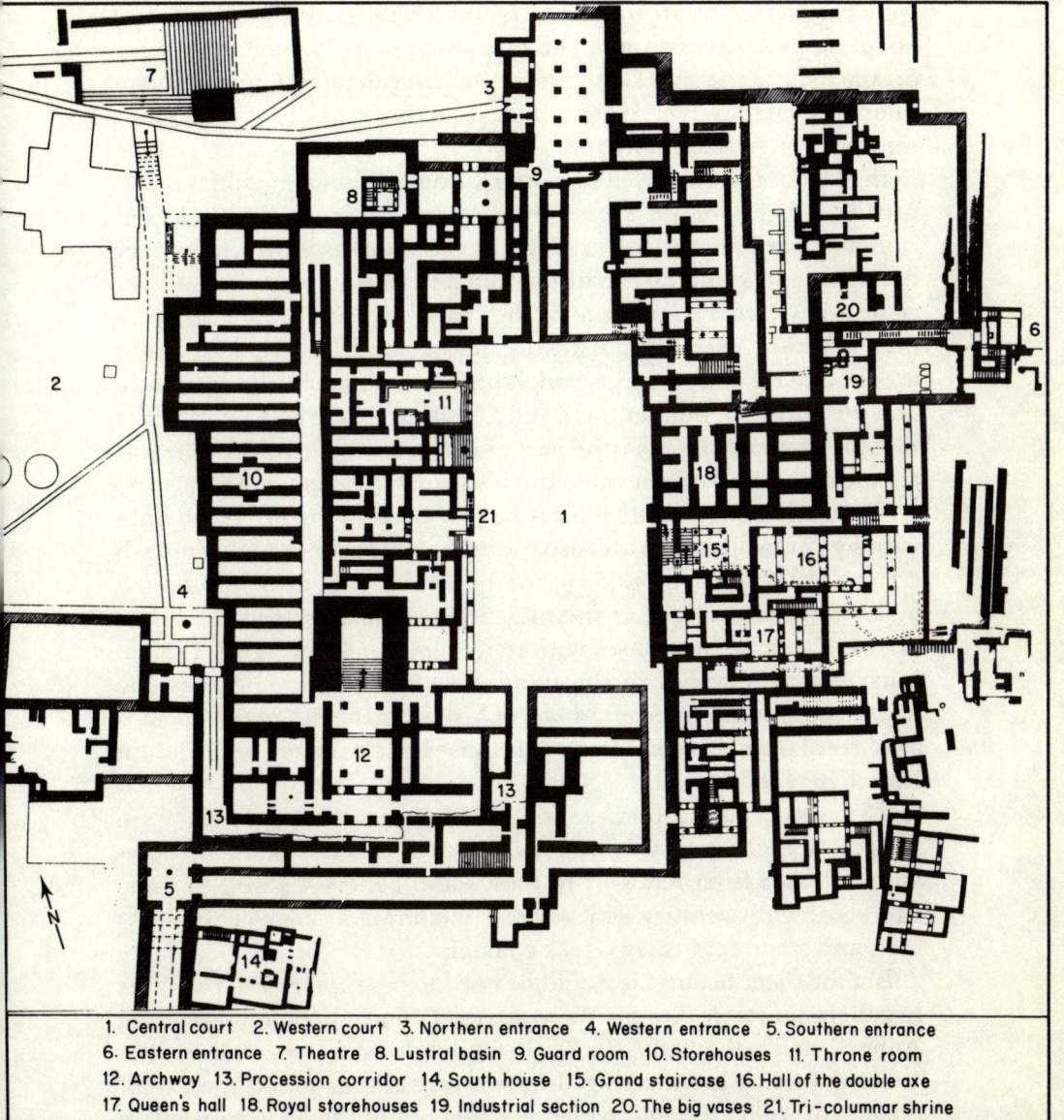

1. Central court 2. Western court 3. Northern entrance 4. Western entrance 5. Southern entrance
6. Eastern entrance 7. Theatre 8. Lustral basin 9. Guard room 10. Storehouses 11. Throne room
12. Archway 13. Procession corridor 14. South house 15. Grand staircase 16. Hall of the double axe
17. Queen's hall 18. Royal storehouses 19. Industrial section 20. The big vases 21. Tri-columnar shrine

Phaestos is decorated with dolphins, and of course there are the marvellous Kamares-style pitchers with spiral designs. But most dramatic of all for many visitors is the famous Phaistos Disc, stamped with characters of an unknown hieroglyphic script, and dated at about 1650 BC to 1600 BC. The disc was found in 1908, and some people believe that it is some sort of ancient calendar. Current scientific thinking, however, is that the text on the disc has some religious significance, perhaps a hymn.

In the fourth gallery, the pottery from Knossos includes vases used in worship of the Sacred Snake, and the Snake Goddess figurines are particularly eye-catching, if only because their mammary development would do credit to a modern pin-up magazine. In the central cases there are some of the finest Minoan finds: the bull's head libation vase from Knossos, jewellery, a royal game board made of inlaid ivory rock crystal, lapis lazuli and gold and silver foil, and the figures of bull jumpers and acrobats. There is the possibility that the ivory acrobat may be part of a larger model, in which he was actually leaping over the bull, and his stance certainly suggests this.

The exhibits in the fifth gallery bear witness to the Minoans' links with Egypt, while there are also examples of Linear-A and Linear-B script. In the seventh gallery, the bronze double axes of Knossos make an appearance, but the most important objects in this room are the Black Steotite vases with relief carvings from Aghia Triada. Each portrays scenes of the daily life of Minoans, and they are classed among the finest products of Minoan art. Also in this room is another of the great treasures of the museum, the honey bee pendant from Khrysolakkas.

The succeeding galleries are devoted to regional finds, from Zakros, Palaikastro, Gournia and Pseira. There are more polychrome vases from Knossos in the twelfth gallery, as well as some superb seventh-century BC jewellery, including a snake chain necklace, and some very early Greek coinage.

But for sheer beauty, it would be hard to beat some of the exhibits in gallery fourteen. Among these are the famous dolphin fresco from Aghia Triada, the 'ladies in blue and dolphins' fresco, and another fresco depicting bull-leaping. In the centre of the room is the Sarcophagus of Aghia Triada, which is made of limestone, is painted on all four sides to show Minoan religious rites for the dead, and is probably the most valuable item in the museum. The remaining galleries are devoted to further fresco pictures, mostly fragmentary, coinage, and statuary which is of some importance in helping to trace the development of Greek sculpture. But don't miss the 'Parisienne' sculpture in gallery fifteen, a fresco which probably depicts a priestess, but was given its extraordinary name by excavation workers who, when they discovered they had found a picture showing a very elegant and sophisticated young lady, compared her favourably with the French fashion models of the day and christened her accordingly.

Besides the Archaeological Museum, the Historical Museum has a collection of art, handicrafts and historical documents dating from the early Christian years to modern times. Some seventeenth-century icons from the monastery of Savathiana, and a painted crucifix from the church of Panaghia Gouverniothissa, are probably the most interesting items, but there is also a good exhibition of Cretan and Aegean dresses and woven fabrics.

Although Knossos is just outside Heraklion, and is easily reached by bus or even on foot, many visitors prefer to join the guided excursions to the site which leave from Heraklion every morning and afternoon. This has many advantages, including the services of a multi-lingual guide, but it is worth considering the alternatives. The local bus services are good, and if you have a self-drive hire car there is ample parking space at the entrance to Knossos itself. The guides are often very good, but linguists will tell you that the stories sometimes vary. And of course joining a coach excursion means that the site will necessarily be somewhat crowded when you arrive. It is often best to go at midday, when, although it can be very hot in summer, there are few organized excursions visiting the site.

Most guide-books suggest that you need at least a day to tour Knossos properly, but the layman will find a half-day visit perfectly adequate. It is a large, rambling site on high land just over three miles from Heraklion. Its setting is such that it cannot possibly have been destroyed by a tidal wave at the time of eruption of Santorini. Evans's reconstruction work, however controversial, does at least give the visitor a very clear idea of the layout of the palace and the circumstances in which the inhabitants once lived. You need a map and a guide-book; the best is Stylianos Alexiou's *A Guide to the Minoan Palaces*, mentioned earlier, although there are also good guide-books and maps, published in various languages, obtainable at the entrance to the site.

Despite the crowds, and the chattering of guides, the site is a strangely peaceful one. Getting around it can be a scramble, particularly if you are trying to find vantage points from which to take photographs. But at least the restoration work, complete with blood-red pillars, makes it a more colourful site than that of most archaeological digs, and the evidence of the Archaeological Museum all helps to bring Knossos alive.

The Palace itself is reached by the west porch, which leads into the Corridor of the Procession, so called because the walls were lined with frescos depicting a procession of people bearing offerings. The upper Propylaeum was restored by Sir Arthur Evans on the evidence of column bases, door jambs, paving slabs and steps which had fallen through to the floor below. From the upper floor, one descends by one of two staircases to the Central Court, from which one should visit the Throne Room, with its gypsum throne and guardian griffins (a mythical beast, part lion and part eagle, from Egypt). The benches which line the walls provided seats for those participating in ritual ceremonies. Many of the rooms are named after the finds which were made there; thus the 'Corridor of the Draught-board' is where the magnificent inlaid gaming board, now to be seen in the Archaeological Museum in Heraklion, was found. Shorn of such items, many of the rooms become meaningless to the casual visitor. But the double-axe symbol is everywhere, as are the bull's horns, carvings of which decorate the outer walls. Rooms to look out for include the Hall of the Double Axes, the Queen's Megaron with its dolphin and rosette frescos and, beyond the Megaron, the bathroom with its clay tub. The corridor leads on to the Queen's Toilet, with its remarkably modern fitments and drainage system.

In the Central Court, the Prince of the Lilies fresco has been restored and replaced on the wall below which the original fragments were found. Nearby, the South House, or House of the High Priest, consists of several storeys and a pillared crypt in a remarkably good state of preservation.

Besides the Palace, there are a number of other buildings on the Knossos site which are not open to the public. In some of these, excavation work still continues.

Visiting both the Archaeological Museum and Knossos itself in the space of one day is one of the highlights of any visit to Crete, but it is also an exhausting process. Refreshments of a rather basic kind can be found opposite the site of Knossos, while there is an excellent *taverna* in the village of Skalani, close by. The road back to Heraklion is also littered with *tavernas*, although the very fact that they necessarily cater for a passing trade, rather than for the locals, makes them suspect. For an evening meal it is better to return to Heraklion itself, where – although good hotels are hard to find – there are at least plenty of restaurants from which to choose. So join the early evening crowds in Plateia Eleutherias or Plateia Venizelon for a quiet drink and some serious consideration of what you want to eat and where you want to eat it. Around the Morosini Fountain, for example, there are a number of *taverna*-style restaurants, offering a choice of either Greek food or rather more international dishes. The restaurant of the Atlantis Hotel, mentioned earlier, also has an international menu, although it should be stressed that in Crete an 'international' menu does not necessarily mean a big choice of dishes, nor a particularly high quality of either preparation or presentation. It really is best to eat out Greek style.

For this, it is important not to go by appearances. Some of the rules for eating out Greek style, and some of the best dishes, are discussed in the later chapter on food, but as far as Heraklion itself is concerned there are some central restaurants (with a peculiarly 1940s appearance) where the food is nonetheless excellent. Fish dishes naturally abound, although if you walk down Evans Street to Theodosaki Street (or 'Dirty Alley') the open-fronted cafes there specialize in charcoal-grilled meat. But the best ethnic-style meal that I have had in Heraklion was in the Castro *taverna*, close to the harbour at the back of the Atlantis Hotel. They have meat or fish on the menu, immense salads soaked in olive oil and liberally sprinkled with white *feta* cheese, and excellent wines. Admittedly the music does tend to get rather noisy as the evening wears on, but that is one of the hazards of eating out almost anywhere in Greece – and the food really does make up for it.

4 The North-East Coast

The motorist touring Crete – a process which requires at least two weeks as well as a fairly tough car and a lot of personal fortitude – almost always seems to choose to go round in a clockwise fashion. Somehow that is the natural route to follow. But the first half-hour or so out of Heraklion is a disappointment, for the new coastal road from Heraklion to the resort of Aghios Nikolaos travels along the north coast past the vast new hotel developments which have sprung up along the beaches, and which are rapidly turning this corner of Crete into a Grecian equivalent of Torremolinos or the Venice Lido.

Ten years ago this road, now the best in Crete, did not exist. Indeed it was along its predecessor that I had my introduction to the island. I had arrived in Heraklion with a friend, a Greek hotelier who had broken her ankle in Athens some days earlier. Because of this we were met by a chauffeur-driven Mini at the airport, and the Greek driver had set out to prove that it was possible to cover the forty-five miles to Aghios Nikolaos in less than an hour, despite the fact that in those days much of the journey was along precipitous mountain roads. For a few miles we followed the flat, uninteresting coastal plain, through 'new' resorts like Malia, and then the road twisted sharply inland and upward. In a few moments we were hurtling along roads which at that time saw little traffic, through tiny villages, round tortuous bends, and along gritty, unfenced lanes clinging to the mountain sides. It was a hair-raising experience and it seemed to go on for ever. In fact, it lasted fifty-five minutes – which gave the Mini driver a great deal of satisfaction even if his passengers did not entirely share this sentiment.

Today the new road means that even the excursion coaches make the trip to Aghios Nikolaos easily in forty-five minutes, and coastal resorts like Malia are within a few minutes' drive of the airport, which is the first point of interest along the road.

Leaving old Heraklion by the site of St George's Gate, the road to the east twists through the suburbs of the city where there are frequent traffic jams caused by selfish parking rather than any great volume of traffic. Greek shoppers follow the habit now practised in some London suburbs and, if they suddenly think of a purchase which they have to make, they stop abruptly outside the shop they wish to visit regardless of who is behind them, and whether or not they are blocking the traffic. There are also less usual habits. On one occasion, driving along this stretch of road, I was halted by a kitten which ran out from a roadside house and lay down in front of my car. When I stopped it did not move; when I got out to move it the kitten, grateful for a little human attention, purred around my legs. While the drivers behind hooted their frustration, I tried to move the kitten to the doorway from which it had run. The occupant of the house, an elderly woman, rapped angrily on the window and the kitten followed me back to the car. Three times I tried to remove the kitten, and three times it came back. Eventually the householder solved the problem by marching out of her front door, grasping the kitten by the scruff of its neck and hurling it over the garden wall. An act of heartless cruelty? Perhaps, but an indication too both of Cretan impatience and – not least – the total mystification which Greeks everywhere share at the British love of animals.

The main road climbs above the airport whilst a branch road leads down to the passenger terminals and huge car parks. It is a busy and crowded airport. Not only does it handle the regular services of Olympic Airways from Athens, and a host of charter flights from all over Europe, but it is also a principal Greek military staging post – a reminder that to the Greeks Crete is considered a 'frontier' area with Turkey.

Beyond the airport, the road drops down to the sea. On your left, stretches of endless sand. On your right the massive Idi and Dikti mountain ranges. But if the beaches look inviting, it cannot be stressed too strongly that there are grave disadvantages to this coast. During the summer, as mentioned before, the *meltemia*, a brisk northerly wind, blows straight on to the beaches, and instead of providing a welcome breeze on the exposed sands is strong enough to whip that sand up into brisk little sand storms. Picnic on one of the northerly beaches during a *meltemia*, and one might quickly think of a new reason why sandwiches are so-called.

Beyond the beaches, the rocky islet of Dia rises from the sea, sharp and barren. Dia is home to a herd of the wild *agrimi* goat, which is unique to Crete. The only place on the mainland of Crete where the *agrimi* goat can now be found is the Gorge of Samaria, which is described later.

Off to the right, a branch road leads to the cave of Eileithyia, goddess of childbirth, which is mentioned by Homer in the *Odyssey*.

The first of the package holiday resorts to be reached is Amnisos, which has fine beaches and a couple of hotels including one of the state-run Xenia hotels which are always a good choice for travellers. This is thought to have been the site of one of the old Minoan harbours, and excavations are continuing on the low hill which rises from the shore. Beyond Amnisos, a hotel development proceeds apace, particularly at Nirou Chani where the Knossos Beach Hotel is probably the best. Beside the lower, or old, road, is a large Minoan villa with a paved front court. A mile farther on, at Gournes, the old and new roads meet, just below a hill crowned by a large radar station. On the coast at this point is the Candia Beach Hotel, whilst a road off to the right leads up to the Plain of Lasithi and eventually down to Neapolis and Aghios Nikolaos – an attractive but very circuitous route to the east coast of the island, which is fully described in Chapter 6 and which motorists should note is not always open.

Just before the resort of Stalis there is one of the all too rare camping sites on Crete, in a magnificent beachside setting. There are only four of these organized sites altogether, two of them on the road between Rethymnon and Heraklion, and one about five miles west of Ierapetra, on the south coast. Camping in Crete is cheap, working out at about half the price of stopping at an official site in France or Italy. The sites do not get too crowded, possibly because many people prefer to camp rough, and simply stop at some roadside spot which takes their fancy. It should be noted that this is officially forbidden, and that you need police permission to camp anywhere but on one of the official sites – although the Cretans cheerfully admit that only one camper in a hundred actually requests such permission.

At Stalis, the Blue Sea Hotel is one increasingly used by British inclusive-holiday firms, and is built in the style which is now so popular on the island, with guests staying in bungalows or apartments which are separate from the main building of the hotel which contains the restaurants, bars and lounges. With its beachside setting, and attractive gardens, the Blue Sea Hotel might be a good holiday choice, the *meltemia* notwithstanding. I also like the Creta

Maris Hotel, seven miles to the west of Stalis and again built in a beachside setting. The Creta Maris has been designed as a Cretan village, and although it stands out in the landscape in a manner which no Cretan village ever did, it would be an attractive holiday choice. One of the disadvantages of this stretch of coast, however, is that along with the new hotels there has sprung up a whole collection of other so-called tourist attractions – ranging from noisy discos to very un-Greek *tavernas* and a series of souvenir shops which not only sell wares which are, to say the least, in dubious taste, but which also push their prices sky high. In most cases you would do far better shopping in Heraklion, or in one of the other main centres, than in one of the tourist-conscious shops along the coastal road.

Beyond Stalis the scenery begins to become more Cretan. Windpumps – skeletal windmills which are one of the commonest sights on Crete – start to dot the landscape, and there are banana groves stretching down to the shore of the Gulf of Malia. At Malia itself, where the old and new roads finally converge, an immense resort seems to be springing up. The attraction here is a truly superb beach, although once again it can be an exposed spot if the *meltemia* is blowing. Around hotels like the Sirens Beach, the Malia Beach, the Belvedere and Icaros Village, a complete town is springing up – a town much favoured by the young and by first-time visitors to Crete who have yet to learn better. But the holiday-makers of today who choose Malia as a destination, are not the first to find this spot attractive. Just outside the new resort lies the old Palace of Malia, which is only of less importance than Knossos and Phaistos. Dating from about 1900 BC, the Palace of Malia has been excavated by the French since 1922. It is good to know that the excavations are in such expert hands, for the site was originally the subject of a sort of latter-day gold rush after the discovery, in the nineteenth century, of fragments of gold leaf there. But the enthusiasm of the treasure hunters who flocked there was somewhat blunted when one of them was crushed to death in a rock fall, and it was only the later chance discovery of some bronze pots and clay sarcophagi near the beach which renewed official interest in the site. Excavation proper began again in 1915, and the discovery of the walls of a large building, Minoan script, and a number of seal stones promised great things to come. Finally, the west wing of the Palace was uncovered, and it was then, for financial reasons, that the French stepped in. A group of Minoan private houses which surrounded the Palace were uncovered and in 1960 the West Court of the Palace was finally revealed, as well as the proto-palatial seal stone workshop and a shrine. To the north of the Palace, pre-palatial graves were found in natural hollows in the soil, as well as the great proto-palatial cemetery of Khrysolakkas, where the famous honey bee pendant was found. Near the Palace, in recent years, a great piazza of the Minoan town has been discovered, as well as a pillared crypt.

Although it is larger than Phaistos, the Palace of Malia seems to have been something of a poor relation to Phaistos and Knossos. Conservation work has been carried out on the finds, but there has been no restoration work of the kind indulged in by Evans at Knossos. The site has thus been preserved largely in its original form. Its proximity to the sea suggests that it was a trading centre, and ships could easily have been hauled up on the nearby beach. But once again, Malia is totally unfortified, and the question remains of quite how the Minoans defended both their settlements and their trade routes. Its position means, of course, that Malia must have been inundated by the massive tidal waves which would have followed the cataclysmic eruption of Santorini.

Tours of the Palace of Malia begin from the West Court, which is paved and divided by a processional way. The southern part of this forks as it approaches a group of circular buildings which were probably granaries. The thick walls suggest that the West Wing of the Palace was originally two-storeyed. The West Storage Magazines are reminiscent of Knossos, but it is noteworthy that no *pithoi* (clay jars) were found here as they were at Knossos, so they must have been removed by the inhabitants at the time of the eruption of Santorini, or destroyed by looters. In rooms nearby were found domestic pottery, a bronze bracelet, a ceremonial axe made of stone shaped like a springing leopard or panther, a dagger, and a superb sword. These finds suggest that this is where the king or priest prepared himself for official ceremonies.

The Loggia is connected with the Central Court by a flight of broad steps. Rooms and chambers close by bear a very close similarity in lay-out to Knossos, and suggest that the rituals performed there must have been almost identical. The sign of the double axe, also reminiscent of Knossos, can be found carved on a pillar in the crypt. There is also a sacrificial altar in the crypt. Steps in one corner of the Central Court appear to have been for spectators watching ceremonies in the court itself, and close to the steps can be seen the famous *kernos* of Malia, a stone vessel containing many small round hollows and a large central one for offerings. This stone seems to have had a ritual purpose, and is still on its original site.

In the south-west corner of the Palace there are silos or granaries, part of the storage system which is a feature of all Minoan palaces. There is a link here with Egypt, where similar stores were built outside dwelling places. There are Magazines in the east wing, where the drainage system suggests that olive oil, grain and perhaps vegetables were stored. In the north wing there is what appears to be a dining-room or banqueting hall, and the remains is of what seems to have been a square, tower-like structure. In the north-west apartments there have been a great many important archaeological finds, including the famous Acrobat's Sword with its hilt sheathed in gold leaf, which is believed to have been set in the ground point upwards in order that acrobats could perform a spectacular – not to mention risky – back somersaults over it.

Beyond Malia the route to the east is suddenly blocked by a mountain range, though the road swings inland through the Gorge of Selenari, where minor traffic-jams and parked vehicles suggest the presence of a road-side cafe, but in fact indicate the presence of something far more important to all true Cretans: an icon. The Holy Icon of St George of Selenari has been placed by the road, and even bus passengers dismount to pay homage to it. The road climbs up to the village of Vrakhasion, tunnels through the 1,310 foot summit, then dips down to the market town of Neapolis, the regional capital until quite recently, and an attractive and picturesque little town surrounded by mountains.

Neapolis is still the legal and ecclesiastical centre of eastern Crete. Its large central square, fringed with pine trees, has the bus station, town hall and post office all situated around it, and the town's museum contains some interesting local antiquities. Many of the houses in the town are particularly grand; Neapolis, one is not surprised to learn, is a popular residential choice for Cretan lawyers, accountants, doctors and other professional men. Because the new road actually by-passes it, it has probably been saved from considerable despoliation, and it has a peaceful and almost romantic air.

The road from Neapolis to Aghios Nikolaos used to be the most hair-raising stretch of the journey from Heraklion, clambering over a couple of minor mountain ranges before finally dropping down to sea-level. But the new road has finished all that. Breaking away from their usual style of road building, which closely followed the contours of the land, the Greek engineers have pushed the new road almost straight through to Aghios Nikolaos, so that you go sweeping through cuttings and over viaducts with nothing more on your mind than the glorious scenery around you. Here the steep green hills and rocky defiles remind one more than anywhere else in Crete of the Highlands of Scotland. All that is missing are the mountain streams – for eastern Crete is a dry, parched land. The new road peters out at a crossroad, three arms of which appear to lead practically nowhere, and turns into one of the stony, ill-defined tracks which comprise most Cretan roads and which the Cretans themselves defend vehemently ('surely it is enough,' philosophized one Cretan to whom I complained about these roads, 'if you reach your destination without destroying your car.') This track drops sharply down to sea-level, and you have to reduce speed quickly, as you find yourself suddenly in the narrow, crowded streets of what has become Crete's most popular, and fastest-growing, resort: Aghios Nikolaos.

5 Aghios Nikolaos

Aghios Nikolaos – a very popular, extremely attractive, and sometimes rather maligned, resort – could not have a prettier setting. A one-time fishing village turned major holiday resort, its white houses tumble down to a harbour which never seems crowded, and beyond it lie the startlingly blue waters of the Gulf of Mirabello. To add to its attraction, the waters from the harbour pass under a narrow bridge and then widen into a deep circular lake in the town centre, fringed on two sides by steep cliffs, on the third side by the town's main thoroughfare, and on the seaward side by a string of bars and *tavernas* with tables set out on the pavement by the edge of the lake. It is an extremely pleasant spot from which to take stock of the town, with peacocks crying harshly from the aviary built on the cliffs, and the youngsters of Aghios Nikolaos splashing happily around in the lake, which they use as a swimming pool.

The town's *tavernas* have been quick to latch on to the popularity engendered by television series featuring Aghios Nikolaos. But the popularity of Aghios Nikolaos has inevitably brought some disadvantages. When I first visited the town, after the drive described in the previous chapter, it was to sink down thankfully at one of the metal-topped tables outside a quayside *taverna*, and order *ouzo* and *mezethes*. Gradually we relaxed. The *mezethes* (snacks of red mullet, slices of octopus, olives, goat's cheese, cucumber, and squares of toasted bread) arrived by the plateful in generous helpings, which I liked to think were offered because I was a stranger (even if that wasn't the reason). The *ouzo*, the soft evening air, the jollity of the *taverna*, the shouted greetings between friends, and the holiday feeling imparted by Aghios Nikolaos all helped to soothe town-taut nerves and to emphasize the unique atmosphere of this big, remote, lovely island.

Things have changed. Today, Aghios Nikolaos is the only place in Greece where young female visitors face the hazard – or perhaps the compliment – of being accosted by local youths anxious for the prestige of being seen walking with or talking to a foreign girl, preferably a blonde. Some of the *tavernas* have renamed themselves after the television series in which they like to think they were featured. Menus have also changed to meet international demand. Such places are fine for a drink, or for indulging in the popular Aghios Nikolaos evening activity of sitting and watching the world go by – or, more accurately, watching the rest of Aghios Nikolaos go by. They are fine, too, if you are tired of Greek food. But to my mind the best meal, not to mention the best value, is offered by the very Cretan Daula *taverna* at the end of the quay – it has the added advantage that on most evenings you can park right outside it, because most visitors will not venture even this far from the bright lights of the town.

The many handicraft and souvenir shops which have sprung up in Aghios Nikolaos stay open late of an evening to cater for the immense holiday traffic. Although it has a population of less than 5,000, in the season this is swollen to two or three times that number because of the visitors staying in the area's many excellent hotels, or in the self-catering accommodation which has sprung up just outside the town. Until recently land was very cheap around Aghios Nikolaos, and many enterprising Cretans have bought plots of land just outside the town, particularly on the road leading towards the village of Elounda, and built holiday villas or blocks of flats. Fortunately these do not intrude too sharply on the landscape; in almost every case the architects have been careful to build in the Cretan style – white houses with enormous archways and inevitably painted in the brightest white – which has also been adopted by some hotel developments. Unfortunately, this has not been possible in the town centre itself. Ten years ago the Hotel Rhea, which can be recommended, was the town's only skyscraper, towering above the other buildings on a hillside site. Today the Hotel Rhea is hard to pick out amid a skyline which has grown as rapidly as the rest of the town; and if this architectural style is international, it is nonetheless to be regretted here in the heart of Crete. But there are advantages; the Hotel Rhea's rooftop bar and restaurant is still a place for a first-class evening out, and the view – particularly at night – is not to be missed.

And, as befits a modern resort, there is plenty to do at night. The main road leading north from the harbour towards the village of

Elounda, Akti Koundourou, is lined with night-clubs and discos offering everything from the latest in western pop music to the strains of *bouzouki* music to which has been added the dubious benefit of electrical amplification. The 'ethnic' night spots are not recommended, if only because the Cretan music which they claim to feature would be unrecognized anywhere else on the island. But at least there is plenty to choose from, and the night-clubs do have the advantage that they have not yet pushed up the prices of their entertainment or their drinks to the levels normally found in a European resort.

Apart from the souvenir shops, the principal shops are to be found on the short but attractively tree-lined Leoforos Koundourou, which climbs from the harbour up to the main square, Platia Venizelou. From the square a narrow street drops down to the other side of the peninsula – and the sea – where the town's busy bus station can be found at the water's edge. The harbour, incidentally, has weekly ferry services to Piraeus and Rhodes.

The town's museum, on the main road out of town to Heraklion, is open from all day on weekdays (although of course it is closed for a few hours for the long Greek lunch hour or siesta), and on Sunday mornings. It is closed on Monday afternoons. Under the curatorship of the charming Costas Thavaras, its eight rooms are arranged around a central court, and they contain early pottery from Myrtos and Mokhlos, finds from burial enclosures at Zakro, some good Late Minoan pottery from Mirsini, jewellery – including necklaces – from the Sitia area, some Sub-Minoan pottery, late finds from the Sitia region including three carved gemstones, and the contents of a Roman tomb unearthed in Aghios Nikolaos itself. The final room contains various exhibits of local folklore. Because this museum is a small one, and because the exhibits are arranged chronologically, it is of considerable interest even to the casual visitor, and throws a great deal of light on the development of the area around Aghios Nikolaos.

Local fishermen will take visitors to the islands of Pseira and Mokhlos, which both have Late Minoan settlements. But a far more popular boat excursion is to the mysterious island of Spinalonga, off Elounda. Once a Venetian stronghold, and more recently a leper colony, Spinalonga is a strange, haunted place. Inside the huge walls of the fortress, Venetian and Turkish buildings remain. One could easily imagine that ghosts linger here too – creaking shutters hang loose and doors bang in the breeze in the street where the lepers lived until the 1950s. The island is like a town from which the population has suddenly vanished, and weeds sprouting from the floor of empty houses proclaim that nature's work of reclamation has begun.

You can see the graves of leprosy victims on the island too, some of them disturbed in one of the rare examples of vandalism which I have ever encountered in Greece. But there is no need to fear, as many visitors do, that you can catch leprosy by visiting the island and touching the remains. Some tourists wash themselves vigorously in the sea after a visit to the island, but in fact there is no fear of infection. The unhappy inhabitants of this island have left no legacy of the dreadful disease which caused them to be outcasts from society; their only legacy is the air of hopelessness and despair which still pervades the island.

Opposite Spinalonga is the tiny village of Elounda, whose inhabitants were once the deadly enemies of the people of Lato, a Doric town, the remains of which can be visited from Aghios Nikolaos (once the port of Lato). But today the natives of Elounda are quite definitely friendly – and they proved it by inviting me to a lunch party at long tables set up in the streets beside the tiny harbour. The Cretans do such things in style; under the benevolent gaze of the village priest, or *papas*, we consumed course after course, washed down with a sweet white local wine, and finishing only as the sun dipped below the horizon. It was a typical example of impromptu hospitality, and one which visitors can share even today in the more remote spots on the island. Such a welcome can be embarrassing, for the hospitality you receive can never be repaid, and even offering to pay for a round of drinks in return may be regarded as an insult. There is no answer to this problem and one must simply enjoy the hospitality and be grateful for it; as the number of tourists increases no doubt it will die away.

Elounda has become famous through the television serial, and book, *Who Pays the Ferryman?* It is a small but attractive village in a fine setting, with some simple accommodation, an increasing number of facilities for self-catering holidays, and a very large choice of excellent *tavernas* specializing in fish dishes. The Britomartis Restaurant, on a quay-side peninsula jutting out into the sea in the centre of Elounda, is run by Ionnis Lyrakis, and is deservedly popular with many visitors. And for a really excellent evening meal, continue along the unmade coast road from Elounda to Plaka (literally: place) where there is a very Cretan *taverna* offering no choice of food – you either eat what the proprietor has cooked (usually fish and really excellent) or you go without. This *taverna* is very popular with the locals, which is always a good guide, and the food is probably without rival in eastern Crete.

On the road between Elounda and Aghios Nikolaos are three of Crete's best hotels: The Minos Beach, just outside Aghios Nikolaos, the Elounda Beach, and the Astir Palace, Elounda. All three are based on a series of bungalows and flats built around a central hotel complex containing such facilities as the reception area, restaurants, bars, lounges and a discotheque; all three are expensive. The Minos Beach was the first of these to be built, in Cretan style, and is still a luxury grade hotel which is deservedly popular with many visitors as well as with the more discerning British tour operators. The Elounda Beach is a personal favourite, with truly superb facilities which, until the hotel moved slightly down-market to attract inclusive tours, made it probably the best hotel in Greece. And the adjoining Astir Palace, Elounda, sets a very high standard of accommodation. All three are distinctive for their huge public rooms (space is one thing which is not at a premium in Crete), and excellent service. At the Elounda Beach I was again a guest at an impromptu party to celebrate someone's 'name day' (Greeks attach great importance to this, and to feting someone called George, for example, on St George's Day rather than on his actual birthday). To the pulsating rhythm of an unamplified *bouzouki*, Voula – the wife of a local architect – and one of the musicians sang the light, amusing, yet strangely haunting Cretan *madinatha* songs, in which the two singers indulge in a 'conversation' made up of couplets played in the same, persistent tempo. To drink there was *raki*, the fiery local spirit that the Cretans deny has anything to do with the Turkish drink of the same name, and which they describe, straight-faced, as the 'Cretan Scotch'. The couple also recited one of the island's favourite poems, which is in praise of a local hero called Barba Panzayios, who did dreadful things to the Turks. During such an evening, it is very easy to start feeling like an integral part of the Cretan scene, and to start toasting the Cretans around you with the word *deknos* – an expression of friendship and brotherhood to which Cretans attach the greatest importance, and to which they will respond with delight.

In the area around the Elounda Beach Hotel a number of wealthy Greeks – plus a smaller number of wealthy non-Greeks – have taken advantage of the development in the area to build themselves very luxurious holiday homes. It is sometimes possible to visit these, for if the owners are staying there, and possibly drinking in the hotel, they are only too delighted to show visitors around the homes of which they are so proud. One holiday villa, built by a wealthy Swiss, and within half a mile of a hotel, is an extraordinary cubic residence built in the form of three self-contained, tower-shaped apartments around a central swimming-pool, and with magnificent marble-floored reception rooms. The owner's idea is that each of her daughters shall, eventually, have a self-contained apartment available in the house. It might be expected that such houses would spoil the ambience of the area – but in fact these rocky hillsides and quiet sandy coves are a long way from being spoilt, if only because they are still the haunt of wandering goats, sheep, and not a few local peasants who are quick to take advantage of the fact that, officially at least, there is no such thing as a private beach in Greece.

6 Around Aghios Nikolaos

Perhaps the principal joy of Aghios Nikolaos is that it is a marvellous touring base. Within easy reach of the town are many of the most interesting and picturesque corners of Crete – ranging from the very typical Cretan village of Kritsa, just a few miles above Aghios Nikolaos, to the extraordinary Plain of Lasithi, which needs a whole day out if it is to be visited properly.

It is an easy afternoon's drive up to Kritsa, where the steep and narrow streets overlook Aghios Nikolaos and the bay of Mirabello. Driving out of Aghios Nikolaos, you turn left at the fork at the crossroad mentioned earlier, the arms of which appear to lead nowhere. In fact the crossroad is part of what is intended to be a sort of by-pass road for Aghios Nikolaos, and the turning to Kritsa is just off the arm leading towards Sitia. As with the entry into Aghios Nikolaos, the road suddenly degenerates from a modern, tarmacadamed road into a country track leading between the olive groves and the fields where Cretan women, dressed in black stockings, colourful skirts and heavy black blouses, load immense panniers of hay or olives on to the backs of patient donkeys which look far too small to move such a load. In fact, these women more often than not load themselves on to the donkey as well, once the panniers are full, and beat vigorously on the beast's hindquarters with a stick in order to get it to move. The sight never fails to draw gasps of dismay from first-time visitors to Crete, but in fact donkeys are, of course, immensely strong and the load is not nearly such a burden to them as it appears. Many of the women are dressed entirely in black, and this indicates widowhood. The long headscarves which they wear are sometimes wrapped around their faces so that it looks as though they are in purdah; but in fact this is to protect their faces against the wind, or the dust on the roads, and when they are working the scarves are worn loose. Peasant women do not always like being photographed, so ask permission first by pointing at them and at the camera. You will get refusals and should accept them gracefully, but as often as not the answer is smiling agreement, the only hazard then being that every Cretan in sight will want to be in the picture and they will arrange themselves into the most formal poses imaginable.

The donkeys, and their passengers, are a traffic hazard on the road up to Kritsa, just as they are on many other Cretan country roads. If the women are accompanied by their menfolk, it is noticeable that the man usually rides the donkey whilst the woman walks behind – another example of the male chauvinism which Cretans accept as normal.

On the way up to Kritsa, one should stop at the thirteenth-century church of Panaghia Kera, a pretty, whitewashed building with a stunted central tower and a separate bell tower, which is set against a backdrop of cypress trees. Unusually, the church has three aisles, and all of them are decorated with fourteenth-century frescoes. The frescoes, considered to be the finest in Crete, have been lovingly restored by the Byzantine Museum in Heraklion. In the south aisle there are scenes from the life of St Anne, the Virgin's mother, St Joachim and the infant Mary. There are scenes from Paradise in the north aisle, whilst in the central aisle the frescoes are devoted to the life of Christ and the Last Judgment. There is a scene depicting the Ascension on the Sanctuary ceiling. The church has a friendly guide, who is there during most of the hours of daylight in summer and who manages to conduct tours of the tiny church which are easily understood by everybody despite the fact that he does not speak a word of any language other than Greek. Perhaps the secret of this is that the magnificent frescoes speak for themselves.

It would be hard to imagine a more typically Greek, or a more attractive, village than Kritsa. Balanced precariously on a hillside, it is a maze of narrow streets and squat white houses with brightly painted front doors and window-frames. Since it was used as the setting for Kazantzakis's film *Christ Re-crucified*, Kritsa has become something of a tourist attraction in its own right, and in the evening it tends to get crowded with excursion coaches which have in turn encouraged the opening of a number of souvenir shops. But at least the souvenirs in question are usually local produce, such as embroidery and crochet work, and the village has not really been spoilt. It is also an extremely friendly place, and every visitor can be assured of a smiling welcome from the villagers whether he has come to spend money or simply to stand and stare. If you have time, it is worth stopping for a drink in one of the *tavernas* on the eastern edge of the village, where balconies built over a sheer drop command a superb view over the Gulf of Mirabello.

A stony track which no self-respecting motorist would use, but along which Cretan drivers roar quite cheerfully, leads from Kritsa to the idyllic site of the seventh-century BC Doric town of Lato. The lack of a proper road has at least protected Lato from the tourist hordes, and it really is a beautiful, if very lonely, place. Set high in the hills, with not a building in sight, the Doric town was built in terraces, and as you climb up these terraces to see the layout of the little houses, the market-place and the Temple, so the view becomes more and more impressive. And as you reach the saddle of the hill, you are suddenly faced with two views: the mountains on one side and, on the other, the steep drop down to Aghios Nikolaos, far below and about eight miles distant, looking like a sort of toy town. In the early evening this view is particularly impressive, and it is worth remembering that Aghios Nikolaos was in fact used by the people of Lato as their port.

Unlike many Minoan towns, Lato was fortified, and although few buildings remain in any identifiable form to a layman's eyes, there is an imposing gate, and the remains of defensive towers, the Agora, and an upper terrace on which stood two altars. Above the Agora there are the ruins of the Temple, which is thought to date back to the fourth century BC. In spring, the site of Lato is carpeted with wild flowers whose perfume fills the air, and the whole atmosphere has that peculiarly magical quality which is unique to the remoter corners of Crete.

Another lonely beauty spot in the vicinity of Kritsa is the Katharo (literally: clean) Plain. A high plateau ringed by mountains, it is notable for its clear atmosphere and eerily total silence. The Katharo Plain is one of those rare spots where it is possible to imagine that you are absolutely alone on this planet.

A longer but more dramatic excursion is to Lasithi, or the Plain of the Windmills. A couple of mountain roads branching off the main road between Heraklion and Aghios Nikolaos climb up to the high, fertile plain, where the sails of thousands of windmills turn silently during the summer months, pumping water on to the potato fields. This really is an extraordinary spot: it has the other-worldly atmosphere that one might expect of some forbidden land in a Victorian novel.

As mentioned earlier, the more westerly of these roads, between Gournes and Malia, is not always open. But I have not known the road from Neapolis to be closed and this is a tortuous if spectacular drive up into the mountains, to a height at which it is impossible to believe that there is a huge, fertile plain above you. En route you pass one or two real windmills (as opposed to windmill pumps) – the tall stone edifices which were once used to grind corn but which are now falling into disrepair. Finally you clear the brow of a hill and the Plain of Lasithi is laid out in front of you – a secret, fertile land. It is not the windmills which catch your eye first, especially as it is usually only in the summer or early autumn that they have sails on them. What is most noticeable, after the drive through a barren, rocky landscape, is the greenness of the plain. Although the many villages here concentrate on growing potatoes, for which the climate and soil are ideal, many other vegetables grow here too, and the plain is like some gigantic market-garden stretching as far as the eye can see. Drive closer, and suddenly you are among the windmills: small, skeletal, metal structures, which do not intrude into the landscape until their white sails are added when they begin their work of pumping water.

Because it is so flat, the plain seems to stretch farther than the five or six miles which it measures in any direction. The windmills are countless – the official figure is 10,000, but the villagers of the plain only laugh if one asks them for a more precise estimate. In fact a count would be impossible; farmers and smallholders are always dismantling rusty old windmills, and erecting new ones in different sites.

If you take the road through Psychro, signs point towards the Dictaean Cave where, as described in Chapter 1, tradition says that Zeus was hidden from his murderous father and spent his childhood. The villagers, anxious to oblige, will tell you that it is an easy walk up to the cave. In fact it is a hard climb needing both the services of a guide and proper footwear, and it takes a couple of hours. There is a tourist pavilion in Psychro, for those who wish to stay in the village and make the climb up to the cave properly.

From Psychro, one can rejoin the road down towards Heraklion – which must make the route through the Plain of Lasithi one of the world's longest short-cuts. It is a dramatic mountain drive, with the great mass of the Dikti mountains glowering threateningly at your back.

Fishermen in the harbour at Heraklion, Crete's main town, working against the backdrop of the Venetian castle.

Shopping in one of Heraklion's busy side streets.

Top Cretan dress varies from the traditional waistcoats, baggy trousers and knee-length boots (left) to more western styles, but they intermingle, as is the case with these two typical islanders.
Above Cretan seascape: the northern coastline to the east of Heraklion.
Opposite Knossos: one of the site's giant storage jars in front of the Bull Frieze Portico.

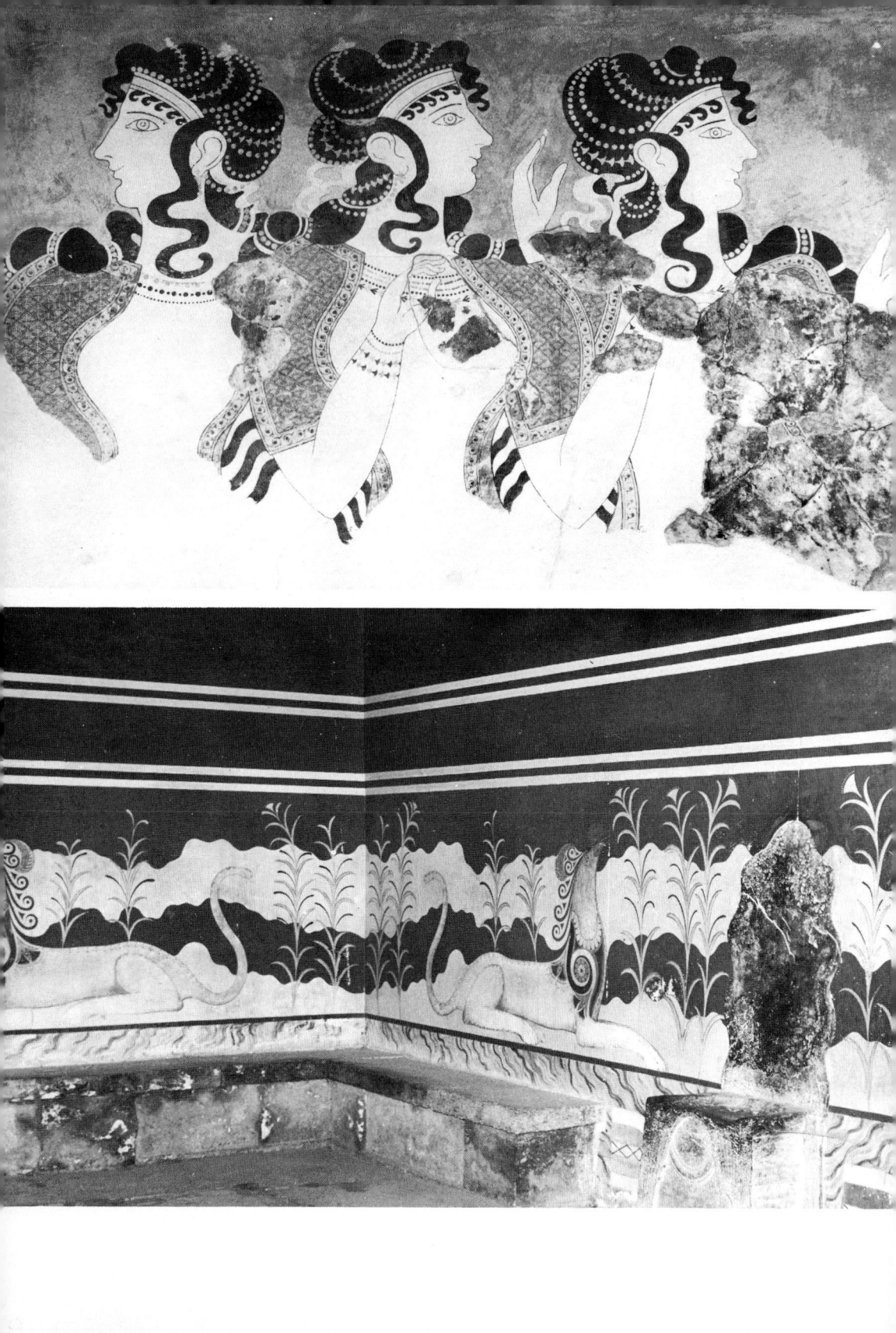

 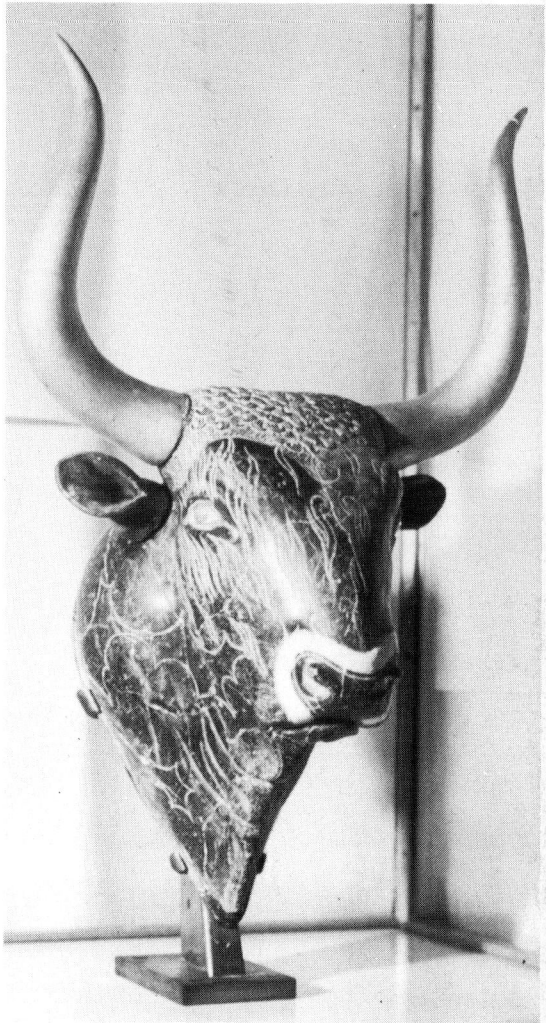

Above opposite The 'Court Ladies' fresco, from Knossos, in the Archaeological Museum, Heraklion.

Opposite Murals in the Throne Room, Knossos.

Above Two of the most famous and popular exhibits in the Archaeological Museum, Heraklion: the 'Snake Goddess' statuette, and the Bull's Head, both from Knossos.

Above opposite The ruins at Malia, on the north coast.

Opposite Still snowcapped at the beginning of summer, the soaring Mount Idi and the Idi range, south-west of Heraklion.

Above Tiny white villages nestling below huge mountains are typical of Crete (this is near Gouria).

The monastery at Arkadi.

Opposite The inner harbour at Aghios Nikolaos, Crete's most popular holiday resort. The tavernas around the harbour and its adjoining lake are the town's lively centre.

Sponge fishermen at Aghios Nikolaos.

Kritsa, one of the most beautiful and unspoiled villages in Crete, is in the hills above Aghios Nikolaos.

The Church of Panaghia Kera, near Kritsa, dates from the thirteenth century and contains the finest Byzantine frescoes in Crete.

Traffic hazard, Cretan style. A country woman riding her donkey just outside Kritsa.

The village of Elounda, near Aghios Nikolaos: an increasingly popular holiday destination.

All in a day's work: a fisherman mending his nets under the tamarisk trees beside the beach at Ierapetra, on Crete's south coast.

Europe's only palm-fringed beach, at Vai, near Sitia.

Souvenirs with a difference: a Cretan shop-front.

Opposite The remains of Aghia Triada, near Phaestos.

Walking through the Gorge of Samaria, in south-west Crete – the longest and deepest gorge in Europe.

There are a number of other half-day excursions from Aghios Nikolaos, to churches rather like Panaghia Kera, in the area around Kritsa. A number of these small churches have frescos, among which the fourteenth-century church of Aghios Georgios Kavousiotis is considered to be the finest.

There is a good, if somewhat twisting, coastal road from Aghios Nikolaos to Sitia, and on to the easternmost corner of the island. Although it is an extension of the north coast motorway, this road has some unusual traffic hazards and passes through some magnificent scenery. After passing through the southern suburbs of Aghios Nikolaos, it hugs the coast of the Bay of Mirabello and passes close to some magnificent beaches, almost all of them deserted even at the height of the season. On the road itself, traffic is often held up by herds of sheep, meandering along guarded by a shepherd or two and perhaps a sheepdog. The shepherds pay no attention to the traffic chaos they are causing, and obviously believe – not without good reason – that in an agricultural community such as this sheep have priority over cars. It is very dangerous for motorists to try to push their way through the flocks of sheep; you just have to be patient and wait until the shepherd leads his flock off the road and into a farm or back on to some mountain track.

The road soon climbs up above the beaches, to follow the rocky coastline in a series of hairpin bends where, despite extensive improvements, the route can still be hazardous and piles of rubble beside the road show only too clearly the danger of rock falls.

About twelve miles east of Aghios Nikolaos, the road reaches the site of Gournia, which is the best preserved Minoan town in Greece. The site was excavated by an American archaeologist, Mrs Boyd Hawes, at the beginning of this century, but although she was a contemporary of Sir Arthur Evans there is none of the reconstruction work which makes or mars Knossos. Founded in early Minoan times, Gournia today consists mostly of late Minoan houses, built along narrow streets. Visitors can walk into these houses, and will notice that they had such up-to-date amenities as running water and main drainage – facilities which are not enjoyed by many Cretans living in village houses today. Stairways connect the streets, and points of interest are the Palace with its Magazines reached by one of these staircases from the open court, and a little shrine in which were found clay tubes with snakes modelled in relief and a clay goddess with raised arms.

But the most extraordinary aspect of Gournia is its hillside position beside the main road. It is practically unmarked, and one could easily drive past it without noticing it. Although it is a magnificent site, it goes almost unremarked on Crete – a reminder that on this island historic ruins and archaeological sites are two a penny. There are more ruined Minoan houses on the other side of the road on the seashore, and these are believed to have been part of the port, which is now under water. You can get a good idea of the ruins by climbing the hillside to the north of the site, from which there is an excellent view. Like Malia, Gournia would have been largely wiped out by the Santorini eruption's tidal waves.

A mile or two farther on the road divides. To the right is the road which crosses the narrowest part of the island and sweeps through rich farmland to the port of Ierapetra, which is described in the next chapter. Even if it were not signposted it would be impossible to miss the turning, for the scenery at this point is dominated by a massive, sheer-faced rock split by a huge chasm. A little way along this road, and almost unnoticed by the roadside, is one of the oldest and prettiest churches in Greece. It stands in the village of Episkopi, and is not even mentioned in many guide-books. Ask in the tiny village for the church, and they will direct you to the modern edifice which stands in the main street. But the far more historic building hides shyly behind a wall at the side of the road almost opposite the modern church, set in a hollow with its roof only just peeping up above road level. It dates from the eleventh century, and its pink-tiled roof crowns walls of dirty white. As often as not the church is locked, but if you can track down the custodian and get inside you will find some very beautiful frescoes and a fine altar. If the custodian is nowhere to be found, as is usual, it is an easy climb on to the roof, at road level, and one can peep through the windows at the tiny interior.

The other branch of the road continues along the coast towards Sitia. At Sfaka a turning to the left leads down to Mochlos, a village opposite a tiny island, with Minoan remains. The island is only a couple of hundred yards offshore, and it is linked by a causeway to the mainland of which it was once probably part. The village itself is a pleasant spot at which to stop for refreshments, although the road leading down to it from Sfaka is somewhat hazardous.

The main road climbs on, around the edge of the Sitia mountains – a small range by Cretan standards but still wild and threatening in the eyes of a visitor to the island. Vineyards cling to the hillsides, and some of the villages along this route, like flower-filled Kavousi, have theatrical hilltop settings on which their churches stand out like beacons.

The twists and turns in the road means that you come upon Sitia almost unexpectedly. It is a pleasant little port, with a big harbour lined with colourful fishing-boats, and dominated by a massive Venetian fort. The Venetians, in fact, had great plans for Sitia, and in addition to the fortress they built a wall around the city. But the latter did not survive the earthquakes which hit the area in 1303 and 1508, nor a raid by the pirate Barbarossa in 1539. The natural rock outcrops around the town are often mistaken for ruined sections of the original walls.

The port is a particularly peaceful spot, and it is lined with a number of good *tavernas* specializing in sea-food. Besides fishing-boats, one may see cargo ships picking up the town's principal export, raisins, and there are occasional ferry services to the neighbouring islands of Karpathos and Rhodes. The B-class Minoa is officially the best hotel in town, but visitors might prefer the C-class Hotel Alice, close to the bus station. It is very quiet, has a sunny roof-top bar with a fine view over the town, and there is a disco in the hotel on one night a week in summer. For meals, you cannot beat the sea-front *tavernas*. The Pegasus is perhaps the best for fish dishes, whilst the unfortunately-named Zorba's *taverna* manages to combine good Greek food in the evenings with a breakfast which will delight the eye of any British visitor: bacon and eggs. Another excellent breakfast in these parts is bread or pastry served with the delicious local honey. And Sitia is still far enough off the tourist track to value its visitors. In the Pegasus *taverna* a waiter who forgot part of one customer's order promptly returned with a free glass of *raki* by means of compensation and apology; while in other restaurants along the quay the staff may calmly take your order and then bring you something entirely different. Their explanation: 'This is the best dish that we have today, and as you are a visitor we thought you ought to have that.' In the city such an excuse would not be acceptable; in a spot like Sitia it is an honest and complimentary gesture that should be appreciated and accepted.

A popular drive is to the isolated monastery of Toplou, which is reached by following the coast road from Sitia, which again passes beautiful and isolated beaches. The monastery, which involves a climb of just over a mile after you have left your car, was founded in 1365, and got its odd name – it means cannon-ball – in Turkish times, when it had a tradition of being one of the centres of island resistance. The monastery contains several fine icons, including the famous 'Lord, Thou are great' painted by the artist Kornaros in 1770 and considered to be one of the greatest masterpieces of Cretan art.

On the eastern tip of the island, below the Toplou monastery and close to Paleokastron, a forest of 5,000 palm trees – the only forest of its kind anywhere in Europe – slopes down to the sea and what is possibly Crete's most famous beach, at Vai. The palm trees are said to have sprung from date stones dropped there by Roman soldiers, but whatever the truth of this legend they are now threatened by local farmers and the monks who covet the agricultural land on which the trees grow; as a result the unique forest is shrinking perceptibly as more and more palms are felled and burned. But tourism may yet perform a work of conservation in this unique corner of a continent. Widespread publicity has made this beach an extremely popular one, especially with young visitors to Crete, and it can be reached relatively easily; it is only about forty minutes' drive from Sitia and is served by about four buses a day in the summer. A great many youngsters camp there, quite illegally, and it is also a popular day excursion. As a result, the felling of palm trees seems recently to have come to a standstill. And if the thought of day-trippers and campers deters you from visiting this beautiful beach, do not be put off; it is large enough to accommodate everyone and there is still plenty of room. Despite its popularity, it remains an extraordinarily peaceful spot, as well as being a very beautiful one with an almost Caribbean appearance.

Paleokastron itself is also the site of a Minoan town, which lies about twenty minutes' walk from the village, going towards the sea. A typical early Minoan house has been excavated there, and the remains of a temple can also be seen.

From Paleokastron, a long and twisting mountain road leads south to Zakro, where it ends in a cul de sac. Journey's end is a tiny village called Kato Zakro, where there is a *taverna* where guests can also stay the night. But the principal sight is the Palace of Zakro, another Minoan ruin which was first excavated at the beginning of the century but has been far more thoroughly excavated comparatively recently. It consists of a terraced town with narrow streets, stepped and cobbled as at Gournia, with a late Minoan palace below. The palace itself is something of a mystery. At some time, possibly when Santorini erupted, it collapsed and burnt, but its inhabitants nevertheless had time to collect most of their belongings and escape before this disaster. It appears as though the inhabitants later returned to Zakro, but the palace itself was never reoccupied, and was not even looted. As a result there have been a number of interesting finds made there, including tablets covered with Linear-A script, friezes of painted stucco, drinking vessels, and goods imported from Cyprus and the Middle East.

Because Zakro is on the road to absolutely nowhere, and a long day's drive from Aghios Nikolaos, it tends to be one of the least visited Cretan sites. The relative unimportance of the surrounding mountains, and the poor (though recently improved) road, are also reasons why it may not feature on many tourists' itineraries. But the beach at Vai should be on everyone's itinerary, and it is worth extending that excursion down to Zakro, even if it does mean spending the night in the village. It is a friendly and attractive spot — where they are delighted to see visitors, and still extend the sort of hospitality for which Cretans are famous.

7 The South Coast

Apart from Aghios Nikolaos, the other main town in eastern Crete is also the only town of any importance on the south coast, where the massive mountain ranges tumbling down to the sea have made both building and any form of local industry hazardous undertakings. It is the small port of Ierapetra, whose principal claim to fame is that it is the most southerly town of any size in the continent of Europe; in fact the shape of the Mediterranean means that it lies far to the south of such better known sunshine resorts as Tunis. Not unnaturally, it accordingly claims for itself Europe's sunshine record – although this is based on local hearsay rather than on any official figures. Local residents wear short-sleeved shirts all year round, report three hundred and forty days of sunshine a year, and claim that you can get a suntan at Ierapetra in January.

I am not able to report on the accuracy of these claims, but the town certainly is a pretty, as well as sunny, resort and it is small wonder that wandering hippies, drawn south as if by magnetic force, ended up here in some numbers a decade ago and took to living on the fine beaches around the town. These hippies, now gone, often seem to act as precursors of tourist invasions, which says much for their taste. But the local people were not amused, particularly when the youngsters moved into cliff-side caves and set up home, and casually-dressed youngsters may still find that they are stopped and questioned about where they are staying, their means, and when they are returning home. You just have to put up with it – or dress more formally.

Ierapetra is in the process of being 'discovered', the number of visitors is increasing every year, and if one had to hazard a guess at Crete's 'resort of the future' Ierapetra would be hard to miss from the list of contenders. It is a lively and attractive town, dominated by the bulk of its Venetian fortress but probably remembered more for its beautiful beach shaded by feathery tamarisk trees, where ancient fishermen sit all day mending nets which they stretch by hooking them on to their bare toes. Accommodation can be something of a problem. The C-class Krita is supposed to be the best hotel in town, but many prefer the Hotel Alice, five minutes from the town centre, which is trying hard to keep up with the latest hotel developments and has even installed an iced water supply. There are also cottages to let in and around Ierapetra.

Of the two main streets, stretching west from the old Turkish town centre (note the minaret and Turkish fountain) the one farthest from the sea is given over to the town's rather simple shops, whilst the sea-front is a cluster composed of bars, *tavernas*, and Spyros Chrissofakis's souvenir shop. Spyros – also known as 'Spyros the Greek', 'Spyros the Barber', and 'Spyros the Golden One' (which is a literal transalation of his surname), but who says with some accuracy, 'There is no need for you to know my name. Everybody knows me' – was indeed the town's barber until a few years ago. It was then that he discovered that not a few visitors to the town were interested in buying as souvenirs some of the sea-urchins' shells, pieces of coral, and other finds which he had made on skin-diving expeditions off the coast of Crete, and which he had displayed on the shelves of his shop. Spyros decided to devote his life entirely to selling these souvenirs, and today his shop is one of the most colourful in Ierapetra – its windows full of shell necklaces, shell brooches, shell key-rings, not to mention the carcasses of a few of the more horrific denizens of the local deep. If it is all in highly dubious taste, that does not worry Spyros, who stands smiling in the doorway of his shop shouting a welcome which cannot be ignored. Show an interest in his wares, and as often as not he will invite you in to discuss any possible purchases over a glass of *raki* or a cup of thick, sweet Greek coffee. These refreshments entail no obligation to buy; Spyros's shop may be a modern manifestation of tourism's more unacceptable face, but his manners and charm are quite definitely part of old Crete.

You can eat well in Andoni's *taverna* and the Psyloyannis Restaurant on the sea-front, which is run by Yamandi and his wife. Meal times at the Psyloyannis can be interesting; I have seen Yamandi's wife chase unwelcome customers from the restaurant with a broom. But whatever she may lack in obsequiousness, she makes up for by her cooking, and if word gets round the town that she is baking the local hot cheese pies known as *misithropitta*, which literally melt in your mouth, queues form at the counter. Also recommended is Thiamando's cafe bar, while there is a bright new disco in town called the Scorpio.

Ierapetra also has a very small museum, next to the Dhimarkhion, which has a fine late Minoan clay *larnax* (urn) vigorously decorated with painted hunting scenes. There are also antiquities from the Roman city of Hieraptyna, which was just outside the modern town of Ierapetra.

If Ierapetra is a friendly place, noted for its excellent food, then the same is true of the coastal villages around it, on the main road which follows the south coast before twisting north towards Sitia. In the village of Ayanis Koutsounari (it means 'big rock' in the Cretan dialect, and refers to the acropolis-like rock behind the village) there is a superb development of self-catering accommodation. A sympathetic Greek developer has taken over the entire village (which consisted of only a dozen or so tumble-down cottages and was used principally by mountain shepherds during the summer months), restored them in authentic Cretan style but with all modern conveniences, then added some matching but very modern cottages and a *taverna*. All the cottages are different, although each one has its own flower-filled garden, and this quiet and secluded spot is ideal for an away-from-it-all holiday whilst still being very close to the fine south coast beaches and to a range of *tavernas* and small village shops selling food and drink. The development is small enough not to be impersonal, and it has also been very carefully planned – in fact the cottages blend so perfectly into the surrounding hillsides that you cannot see Koutsounari until you are almost upon it.

Above Koutsounari can be found one of Crete's typical mountain villages: Aghios Ioannis. The road – track would be a better word – leading up to Aghios Ioannis twists tortuously around what feel like mountain tops but which are in fact the lower slopes of the Sitia mountains. It criss-crosses the stream which led to the siting of the village in the first place, and eventually, after a half-hour drive during which you cover practically no distance at all as the crow flies, you reach the out-lying houses and smallholdings, where as often as not the villagers will stop your car to shout greetings. One of these villagers engaged me in a long conversation about traffic hazards on the road and, despite the fact that there probably had not been a car through the village for at least a week, shook his head sadly over such modern developments and pointed proudly to his own transport which he said was infinitely preferable, not to mention far cheaper to run. The transport in question turned out to be a couple of sprightly looking donkeys.

In the village itself, visitors are sufficiently rare for people to stop and stare quite openly at any outsiders – although this is entirely out of curiosity and nothing else. In all probability, youngsters will run to report your presence to the mayor, and if he is not working or enjoying his siesta he may appear to have a formal drink with you – stopping only to put on his chain of office. It does not matter that he does not speak a word of English, and you may not speak a word of Greek; he merely wishes to extend the town's hospitality to you and bid you welcome. It is a very charming gesture and one which should not be ignored. The road back down to the coast from Aghios Ioannis is hazardous because of the loose gravel and also because (particularly at night) the rocks and boulders which often strew the road cannot always be seen very easily.

The new coastal road from Ierapetra to Timbaki, part of a top-class road intended to encircle the island, but not yet complete, runs briefly along the coast before climbing through the Dikti mountains. The first village of any note on this route is Pefkos, then the road drops down into a couple of valleys before climbing again to Ano Vianos, a village surrounded by vineyards and olive groves. This is the real Crete, a hard country peopled by stern men who still carry rifles, and by shy, self-effacing womenfolk.

Perhaps history is to blame, but here in the mountains the carrying of arms is equated with manliness, just as is the revenging of any dishonour upon oneself or one's family, and despite Greek laws banning arms many peasants carry either a rifle or a shotgun, and even the apparently unarmed youngster may have a knife in his belt while grey-suited businessmen may pack a pistol in their pockets. Not surprisingly, the Germans found these mountain areas particularly hard to subdue during the occupation of Greece in the Second World War, and guerrilla fighters who had fled into the mountains they knew so well used to emerge to attack German outposts. The Germans responded by indulging in wholesale retribution against the villages accused of harbouring guerrillas. There is a memorial at Ano Vianos to victims of the occupation; other villages in these mountains were completely razed, or else saw the male inhabitants taken as hostages and, not infrequently, shot.

The village of Ano Vianos is crowned by the little church of Aghia

Pelayia, where the frescoes date back to 1360. You can stay in Ano Vianos, but many tourists prefer to take the poor road which turns off the main road between Ano Vianos and Pefkos, and leads down to the coast at Arvari, where there is an inn, a good beach, and a spectacular gorge running down to the sea.

From Ano Vianos, one of the few roads crossing Crete in a north-south direction winds its precipitous way through the large village of Kastelli to join the main north coast road near Gournes. En route, both Kastelli and neighbouring Pigi have Byzantine churches with well-preserved frescoes.

The road from Ano Vianos continues west through Pirgos – set in the Anapodiaris Valley, which is separated from the sea by the coastal Asterousia mountains, – Charakas, and Mires to the beautiful archaeological site at Phaistos, where a Minoan Palace, second in importance only to the one at Knossos, has been uncovered, and Aghia Triada. But before one reaches Phaistos and Aghia Triada, look out for another of the turnings off the road, just before Aghi Deka, which is the main north-south road in Crete. Up this road, on the way to Heraklion, is the village of Aghia Varvara, where the tiny church of Prophitis Elias, set high on a rock, is said to mark the exact centre of Crete.

Close to Aghi Deka, a village named after ten martyrs said to have been executed on a stone now in the Byzantine church in the village during a Roman persecution, is Gortyn, the old Roman capital of Crete. This is a pleasant spot to stop and explore at leisure, with pride of place going to the Roman Odeon, behind which can be found the famous Code of Laws, said to be Europe's first written code of law. Gortyn dates right back to Neolithic times, and Homer referred to it as a walled city, although no walls survive today. The Code of Laws dates from about 500 BC, when Gortyn was part of a group of allied cities in Crete. After the Roman conquest, Gortyn was made the provincial capital, and most of the buildings now to be seen date from the second century AD. But the Romans re-erected behind the Odeon the eight vast carved tablets, written in a form of Dorian dialect, which make up the Code of Law. Translations show that it concerns the crimes of, and punishments for, such offences as assault, adultery and divorce, as well as such civil matters as land tenure and inheritance. The Acropolis, opposite the Odeon, is the site of the original Neolithic and Early Minoan settlements.

At Mires, a road climbs up from the plain to cross the southern mountains and descends again to the fine beach at Kali Limenes, a little known resort. There is another fine beach at Matala, which is reached by taking a turning off the main road between Mires – a colourful market town – and Timbaki.

Matala has recently replaced Ierapetra as a haven for the hippy community, again attracted by the fine beach and the abundance of caves. And, true to form, the more usual holidaymakers are following the hippies' choice of resort, but staying in such new hotels as the Matala Bay Hotel which boasts good rooms, spacious lounges, both Greek and international cuisine, and what it quaintly describes as a 'distraction space' for children. But if visitors to south coast resorts like Matala think that they are going to escape the *meltemia* they may be in for a surprise; the south coast has its own irritating summer winds in the shape of the North African *sirocco*.

Matala is, of course, very convenient for visiting the Palace of Phaistos, magnificently situated on a hill overlooking the rich Messara Plain around Mires. Phaistos is smaller and less imposing then Knossos, but nonetheless important. It has a tourist pavilion and museum nearby.

An English naval officer, Captain Spratt, first recognized the site of ancient Phaistos when he was travelling in Crete in the 1850s. The city contributed ships and men for the Trojan War, and Homer describes it as 'well populated'.

Some early Minoan finds nearby, and a reconnoitre of the site by the Italian archaeologist Federico Halbherr in 1884, directed further attention on the site, and in 1894 Halbherr returned to Phaistos and discovered some fragments of Kamares ware. The hunt was on and, as in the case of Knossos, the final expulsion of the Turks, and the proclamation of Cretan independence in 1898, gave the Italian archaeologists the opportunity for which they were waiting. A systematic excavation, directed by Halbherr, began.

There was some work of maintenance and restoration, but – unlike Knossos – this was done only when there was absolutely no doubt about the original appearance of the features in question. The Palace had been completely excavated by 1908, although work on adjoining buildings continued right up until 1939. After the Second World War a new series of excavations was carried out by the Italians under the direction of Professor Doro Levi, revealing parts of the Old Palace and some splendid examples of polychrome Kamares pottery.

The layout of the Palace shows a great similarity to that of Knossos, with rooms grouped round a large, paved Central Court and various areas apparently designated for such purposes as religious and cult practices, workshops, storage etc. Tiered rows of seats were provided in the West Court, presumably for spectators at religious or other ceremonies, whilst a group of small rooms at the foot of the Grand Staircase is where many of the objects now on display in the Archaeological Museum in Heraklion were found. The Grand Staircase leads up to the Propyleion, below which many of the Kamares vases were found. Another staircase leads down to the huge Central Court, off which there is an almost square pillared hall and more storage Magazines. Also to be seen are apartments that are believed to have belonged to the king and queen, which could be linked together or partitioned off. Domestic apartments, away from the main rooms, are where a number of Late Minoan vases and some bronze double axes were found.

The fate of the Old Palace is clear enough even to the layman: blackened walls and charcoal bear witness to a destructive fire, after which the New Palace came into its own. Whatever fate befell the other Minoan palaces on Crete was shared by Phaistos, although pottery finds, and the lack of any Linear-B script, indicate a later reoccupation than occurred elsewhere. What reoccupation there was seems to have been on an individual basis, perhaps by wandering Mycenaeans, and the town survived the Doric conquests in 1100 BC. To later occupation of the site belongs the Temple of Rhea, close to the Palace, where bronze fragments were found. The town flourished until about 180 BC, when it appears to have been destroyed by neighbouring Gortyn. It was rebuilt yet again in Roman times, but the Roman and Hellenistic remains had to be removed to enable archaeologists to get at the Minoan remains beneath them.

Only about three miles from Phaistos is the site of Aghia Triada, named after the double-naved Venetian church almost next to it and beautifully situated among orange groves overlooking the sea. A number of Middle Minoan and Late Minoan villas have been uncovered here, in what was obviously a major Minoan town.

Off the open, paved Court is a rectangular shrine which was decorated with murals now in the Archaeological Museum in Heraklion. Artefacts similar to those from Gournia were found in the shrine, and a fine bronze double axe was found beside it. A two-storeyed villa, also known as the Small Palace, shows both residential and storage rooms, and superb frescoes found on the walls (now in Heraklion) included a woman sitting in a garden and a cat stalking a pheasant. Graffiti on the walls is in Linear-A script.

The main street leading towards the sea, the Rampa del Mare, has the remains of Middle Minoan houses beside it, and a staircase leads down to the Late Minoan Town area, which had both shops and warehouses. In the cemeteries, close by, are the remains of two circular stone *tholos* (dome-shaped) tombs, and finds here have produced strong evidence of Egyptian influence in the city.

Although many visitors to the Phaistos and Aghia Triada sites choose to stay at Matala, a far better bet would be Aghia Galini, a tiny, unspoilt fishing village which is reached by a twisting track leading off the main road back towards Rethymnon. Hidden in a cleft in the cliffs, Aghia Galini consists of a little harbour full of fishing boats, a stately stone staircase, a town square with a fountain, and a handful of houses. Its three *tavernas* are all excellent, but compete vigorously for custom, with the proprietors insisting that the stranger should try a little of everything. They serve *ouzo* and *retsina*, of course – but have also been known to serve up gin in half-pint mugs filled to the brim. You can stay with village families very cheaply, or put up at the Acropole Hotel. The only telephone is in Costas's fascinating shop, which sells – according to the notice outside – 'postcards, stamps, bacon, eggs, and notions.'

8 Rethymnon

The coastal road from Heraklion to Rethymnon and Chania in the west of the island is the busiest in Crete, with lorries full of local produce trundling to and from the ports, and regular bus services ferrying islanders from their villages to the shops and back again.

A little way outside Heraklion along this road is the Akti Zeus Hotel, a new first class hotel, built, so the owners claim, in the style of a Grecian monastery. It is certainly a good holiday hotel, with a great many facilities.

But before reaching the hotel, a road turns off to the left and up into the Idi mountains. You climb through olive groves, which soon give way to vineyards, and finally up into the hard, stony country grazed first by sheep and then, as you get higher, only by goats. The black slate beehive-shaped huts at the roadside are used for storing cheese, and the temperature inside remains constant.

After climbing through a number of small villages the road finally crosses over a saddle of mountain which acts almost as a giant protective wall. Then it swings into the large village of Anoyia – where the long street of cubic-shaped houses bears little relation to the architecture of any other town or village in Crete.

The reason is simple enough. On 13 August 1944 5,000 German soldiers marched into Anoyia, dragged the town's 2,500 women and children out of their houses, systematically burnt every one of the 940 buildings, and then dive-bombed the village. Anoyia was completely razed, and only the church was left standing.

This act was one of the frequent German reprisals against the activities of the various partisan groups who operated in the mountains of Crete throughout the German occupation, and was also the most comprehensive – if not the cruellest – of these reprisals. Many villages in southern and western Crete suffered a similar fate, and as often as not hostages – usually males, but occasionally women and children – were taken out in groups and shot. It was one of the few ways in which the Germans could fight back against the activities of the partisans who, besides passing information to the allies and assisting with commando raids, had helped the many British and Commonwealth soldiers left on the island after the evacuation of Crete in 1941, and persisted in launching raids against the German supply lines and against isolated military targets.

The destruction of Anoyia was in part a general act of retribution for the activities of the partisans. But it also came at a time when the Germans were still smarting from the capture and abduction of their commandant on the island, General Karl Kreipe, who had been kidnapped by a group of Britons and Cretans in late April 1944 and spirited out of the island to Egypt. (The tale of this kidnapping is well known, having been related by one of the Britons involved, Stanley Moss, in his book *Ill Met by Moonlight*, which was also made into a film.) The capture of General Kreipe was one of the highlights of allied activity on Crete during the occupation, but German reprisals were terrible. They rounded up and shot almost every Cretan man that they could find, and burnt or blew up no less than eight villages, on the northern slopes of the Idi mountains. Many Cretans believe that, in retrospect, the escapade was not worth the terror which it invoked.

Anoyia was by far the largest village to be thus destroyed, but in some respects it seems to have got off fairly lightly. Those males who were not actually fighting in the Resistance had long ago learned that it was safest to sleep rough, up in the mountains, whilst the Germans were on the rampage, and they all escaped. Some villagers claim today that many of the women and children were in fact shot during the destruction of the village, but I have been unable to trace any official record of this, and it seems unlikely that an atrocity of this magnitude would go unrecorded. Be that as it may, Anoyia today bears the strangely unsettled air of a refugee camp, with its sad, new houses and its oppressive atmosphere. The villagers are naturally reluctant that their village should be any part of the tourist trail through Crete, and strangers are not made welcome – or at least not until they have identified themselves, and their nationality. A *taverna* owner in the town ignored me when I went in for a drink after the drive up from Heraklion, pointedly turning his back until I spoke to him in English. When he turned round, I was joined at the counter by a Cretan wearing the island costume of full-sleeved shirt, embroidered waistcoat, cummerbund, baggy trousers and knee-length leather boots, and leaning heavily on a stick. He was proud to own up to having been a Resistance fighter, yet spoke sadly, and with a far-away look in his eyes, of the war which had caused so much devastation to his home. When we shared a drink, his eyes brightened a little. The hills he fought through, he said, he now herded sheep through – and at least it kept you fit. To prove it, he put his knarled, weather-beaten hand in mine, and squeezed, inviting me to return the pressure. For a moment our hands strained against each other and then he smiled and tightened his grip as easily and powerfully as a mechanic's vice. Just as I thought the bones were about to start cracking, he smiled again, triumphantly, and let go. Would I like to know how old he was, he asked. I said that I would. Seventy, he replied. He had made his point.

The men of the Idi mountains, like those of Sfakia, that ill-defined mountain area to the west, live hard but still value their sort of life sufficiently to fight and die for it. Indeed, one is almost tempted to wonder why such a succession of unfriendly visitors have seemed determined to try to subdue them. They might have learnt their lesson as long ago as Turkish times, when the Turkish occupying forces decided to collect taxes from the Sfakia region. Every time a tax collector went up into the mountains, the Sfakians killed him. Eventually, the Turks – faced, no doubt, with a shortage of tax collectors – decided that it was not worth the trouble and left the region untaxed.

The road from Anoyia runs down through the large village of Perama to rejoin the coastal road. But a few miles farther on towards Rethymnon a road off to the left climbs up through the olive groves and a rocky gorge to what is still perhaps the most emotive spot in Crete: the monastery at Arkadi.

Arkadi is to all Cretans what Masada is to the people of Israel. Here, in the purple mountains high above Rethymnon, the seventh-century monastery was the scene of an appalling climax to the running battle between the Cretans and their Turkish overlords in the nineteenth century. During the fighting, in November 1866, a large number of Cretan men, women and children from the surrounding villages took refuge in the monastery as the Turks brought up an army of several thousand men to do battle with the Cretan guerrillas. The Turks laid siege to the monastery, in which a large quantity of explosives had been stored by the guerrilla fighters. Faced with the awful choice between surrender to the Turkish troops (and probably slaughter at their hands) or using the explosives to destroy the monastery, the Abbot Gabriel chose the latter, blowing up not only the monastery and its defenders and refugees, but an estimated 3,000 of the opposing Turks. The incident, on November 7, is still commemorated every year as a national holiday in Crete, and it also gave rise to the motto which is still a Cretan password: Freedom or Death.

The church suffered most in the explosion, and has been restored. But the monastery itself is today a sad and almost deserted place, housing only nine monks. They will happily show visitors relics of the destruction of Arkadi, including the Abbot Gabriel's vestments which have been preserved. And they will also offer you a snack of olives, brown bread, and homemade *raki* which is called *tsikoudia*.

The port of Rethymnon itself somehow manages to look as though it is still suffering from the visitation by Turkish pirates who burned it in 1571. Once fortified, it still has vestiges of grandeur, tourists will see it as an attractive town with rows of pretty houses often decorated with iron balconies. *Tavernas* ring the small fishing harbour, while ferry boats use a bigger and far less attractive harbour.

Besides the forces of the Turks, Rethymnon has suffered from occupying forces of Romans, Saracens, Spanish Arabs, and of course the Venetians. But the city flourished during the period it was occupied by the Venetians, and despite their cruelty to the inhabitants the Venetian influence has left its mark on the city architecturally. Apart from the Venetian fortress, the 'Fortezza', and the Venetian Loggia, look for the Venetian Niche with its coat of arms and the Venetian inscription at 35 Emmanuel Bernardou Street; the Venetian Niche at 44 Arcadiou Street; the facade of a Venetian building at 46 Arcadiou Street; and the four Venetian gates.

Another surviving example of Venetian architecture, in the main street of the town, is the Arimondi Fountain, which dates from 1623. Alvise Arimondi was a Venetian who built a number of fountains around Rethymnon, and the surviving one boasts four Corinthian columns. The wall at the back of the fountain dates from the Turkish period, and has been restored.

Rethymnon, which is situated almost half-way between Heraklion and Chania, also has a tradition of being the intellectual centre of Crete. In the words of Pandelis Prevelakis, the well known writer and Professor at the School of Fine Arts in Athens: 'It is said that once the town enjoyed the reputation of being renowned all over the world for the importance of its commerce and excellent sailors. This town also gave light to two or three good painters and poets thanks to whom the glory of the town perpetuates through the ages when its prosperity declines, its arsenals are abandoned and its best children have emigrated at a very fast rhythm.

'It is also said – something that can be easily checked – that the citizens of Rethymnon were kind, modest but at the same time proud, educated, good mannered and peace-loving; briefly, a rare species in the rather turbulent island.'

Certainly, the town, which today has a population of about 16,000, has produced more than its fair share of intellectuals. And, since the sixteenth century, Rethymnon has given precedence to the intellectual movement, especially the arts. Its sons include the sixteenth-century editor of the Greek classics and lexicographer, Markos Moussourosa; the seventeenth-century poet Antonios Ahelis; the eighteenth-century poet and dramatist Georgios Chortatzia, and a handful of other eighteenth-century poets; the Kallergis family of academics; the writers and educationalists Ioannis Damborgis, Efstratios Fotakis, and Michael Prevalakis; and the poet Georgios Kalomenopoulos, many of whose verses are about the city. It has also produced a great many university professors who have become giants of Greek letters.

Probably as a result of these links, such associations and guilds as the Lyceum of Greek Women and the Historical and Laographical Society have their headquarters in Rethymnon. The tradition is such that many artists and intellectuals are now given government aid if they wish to live or work in the city. And, in the glowing words of an official Greek government hand-out, 'The thirst now for learning that characterizes the Rethymnians necessitates the existence of many schools. All these, tradition, institutions, schools and the human element create in Rethymnon an atmosphere of tranquility and humane-ness.' It may be that this interest in the arts has been spurred by the fact that Rethymnon has always been in the shade compared with its neighbour, Chania, when it comes to the quality which Cretans undoubtedly admire most: fighting. But I suspect that the city's ambience, its wealth of well preserved historical buildings, and its attractive tree-lined streets have much to do with it. It would be a pleasant place in which to live and work.

The city has made little effort to attract tourists and tends to keep itself to itself, living with the memories of the past which are re-lived through the maintenance of ancient customs and traditions. But an increasing number of visitors are, quite literally, discovering the city. It is a very attractive town to explore, and no-one can fail to be moved by their first sight of the Fortezza, which was built in 1574, or the view from the Fortezza over the town to the sea and the picturesque Venetian harbour. Narrow little streets, old houses, stony gates, Venetian fountains, kiosks, Turkish minarets, mosques . . . and even that rarity on Crete, a municipal gardens bright with thick vegetation and brilliant flowers. Rethymnon has them all – and it can even claim another rarity on Crete: a tiny zoo. Here, among other animals indigenous to the island, can be seen the wild *agrimi* goat, or *kri-kri*, which (as mentioned before) can nowadays normally be seen in the wild only on the islet of Dia or, if you are very lucky, in the Gorge of Samaria.

On the main street of the town also stands the Loggia, one of the most Venetian buildings in Crete, now housing the Archaeological Museum in which there are finds from all over the province of Rethymnon, including Minoan, Classical and Roman remains and artefacts.

The Fortezza, the city's most impressive structure, is built on a rocky promontory on the coast. In fact the headland was once virtually an island, and the city of Rethymnon is built on the isthmus leading across to the Fortezza. The first fort on this site was ruined by marauding Turks in 1571, and was rebuilt and enlarged to include the Cathedral of St Nicholas, the Rector's Palace, and other buildings. All of these were allowed to fall into ruin after 1646, when the Turks finally occupied it. What the Turks did not despoil the Germans did, during the Second World War, when the Fortezza suffered from aerial bombardment. But the massive walls are still largely intact, as is the main gate which is seen at its best when entering from the town.

Unusually for a Cretan resort, Rethymnon has a well organized beach, centrally situated, which is protected from the winds and is kept very clean. You pay a modest fee to use this beach, but as it has changing rooms and a snack bar this is worthwhile. There is another very good beach about twelve miles to the west of the town, the sandy Petres River Beach.

There are plenty of small hotels in and around Rethymnon, of which the A-class Rethymna, laid out as a bungalow complex, is the best. Other good hotels include the bungalow-style Lavris, the Ideon, the Valaris (close to the bus station, and especially recommended), the El Greco and the government-owned Xenia. Crete's oldest camping site, Camping Elisabeth, is a couple of miles out of town on the road to Heraklion, and is well situated.

For a meal of fresh fish, and Cretan *ouzo* or *raki*, there are a number of picturesque little *tavernas* surrounding the Venetian harbour. Alternatively the town has several very good restaurants and bars which provide an authentic taste of Cretan cooking. These include the beach-side Macedonia, Kyrianitakas Tsakali and Zambetakis restaurants, and the Lemonakis restaurant at Heroon Square. Crayfish are a speciality of the town, but are expensive.

Because Rethymnon is so centrally situated, there are a number of fascinating excursions to be made from the town, either by bus or by car. The bus services from Rethymnon are excellent. Crossing the Gorge of Kourtalioti, for example, one can visit the Preveli monastery, then go on to the tiny seaside village of Plakia, where there is a very good beach and some sea-front *tavernas* offering the freshest of fish, and comfortable beds for the night. The route back to Rethymnon includes another huge gorge, the Gorge of Kotsyfos.

There are excursions to Anoyia, from which it is possible to continue up to the vast Idi Cave, which – along with the Dictaean Cave – is claimed to be where Zeus spent much of his childhood under the care of a goat. The people of central Crete, in an argument which it is typically impossible to resolve, insist that the Idi Cave is where Zeus was actually born and hidden by his mother – but students of ancient Greek myths prefer to place this event in the Dictaean Cave.

In the picturesque village of Roustics there is a very old monastery which sees relatively few visitors; and the same can be said for the villages of Episcopi, Argyroupolis – with its abundant waters – and the ancient city of Lappae. Farther south, the village of Myriokefala has an icon of the Virgin Mary which is said to be capable of working miracles, a familiar claim in Greece, as well as a comfortable guest house.

A word should be said at this point about Crete's wealth of historical monasteries. Most of them were founded during the first Byzantine period, and especially the last centuries of the Venetian occupation. At that period the religious feeling of the Cretan people was at its peak, not only for religious reasons, but also because of the sense of unity which it brought to an occupied island.

Cretans could not bear the thought of serving in the Venetian army, in which the hardship was considerable and in which, in any case, many soldiers going abroad were destined never to return. To escape this fate many of them became monks, which enabled them to avoid military service.

But these self-same monasteries still fulfilled a military role. Some of them were built on fortified sites, deep in the heart of the Cretan countryside and away from the inquisitive eye of the occupying Venetian forces. They became centres of local resistance, which is why many of them were subjected to the long sieges which caused damage or complete ruin to them. They also served as centres in which the island's language and character, as well as the Greek Orthodox religion, were preserved. However, the serenity of the monasteries, the environment and the daily contact with books meant that the monks did have an academic role too, so that the inclination for learning increased, and many of the monasteries became centres of teaching and knowledge.

With the decline of the Byzantine empire, and the fall of Constantinople in 1453, Crete became a refuge for artists and scholars from the Greek mainland, and one of the last outposts of Orthodox Greek culture. Orthodox monasteries, schools, literature and painting flourished in Crete, borrowing details from the Venetians but essentially preserving Greek traditions. Teachers flourished in such profusion that for a time they even became a famous Cretan export – with both islanders and those who had fled to the island and studied there moving on to other centres of learning in western Europe and helping to preserve, and spread, Greek culture.

Mediaeval-Renaissance Crete has long been seen as a centre for the painting both of frescoes and icons. The 'idealistic school' of Constantinople, and the 1,000 years of art that had flourished in Byzantium, was preserved in Crete after the fall of the Byzantine world. A new school called the Cretan School, formed on the island in the fifteenth and sixteenth centuries, constituted the most important period of Greek painting after the fall of Constantinople.

It was during the Turkish occupation of Crete that the Greeks, through their art, explored not only their religious world but also their national conscience. The 'Cretan school' refers to the fresco painting that flourished during the fifteenth and sixteenth centuries, although frescoes of other periods – as well as icons of that era – reveal some of the same spirit. In the sixteenth century several Cretan painters worked on the Greek mainland, so that works of the Cretan school are still to be seen in the monasteries of Mount Athos and the Meteora. Icons, rather than large-scale frescoes, became a Cretan speciality. The tradition was a long one: Cretan icons can be found dating back to the fourteenth century. The tradition was given a more modern touch when the Cretan master Michael Damaskinos returned to Crete after a long spell in Italy and blended his Italian-Renaissance style with the Byzantine style in his major works, executed between 1570 and 1591. His six famous icons now to be seen in the Cathedral of St Menas in Heraklion were once in the Vrondisi Monastery.

The final bridge between the Byzantine and western art forms, however, as well as between the mediaeval and modern worlds, and between the Orthodox and Catholic traditions, was Domenico Theotokopoulos, or 'El Greco' (1541–1614). None of his work is to be seen in Crete, but Crete is to be seen in much of El Greco's painting.

Among the six hundred or more chapels and churches on Crete, there are still many that have their wall paintings intact, and many of these have been painstakingly restored. Icons from the Damaskinos era are to be found in a number of Cretan monasteries. They are always worth seeing, and somehow add to the mysterious, yet peaceful, ambience of these remote religious centres. As has been mentioned earlier, the visitor is always sure of a welcome at a Cretan monastery, where the monks will willingly share their frugal meals and even more basic accommodation. But look again at these monks, for they are the men who were largely responsible for keeping Crete as it is today. They not only knew how to burn incense, but also how to burn gunpowder when the need arose. Their candles kept alive the hopes of liberation while the island suffered its long period of slavery under the Venetians and Turks. It was in the monasteries, during Crete's fierce struggle for independence, that the monks taught Cretan children to read and write the Greek language – which was prohibited by the Turks – at schools where the children studied in secret and only by the light of the moon.

Finally, from Rethymnon there is the popular excursion into the Amari Valley which, despite being a valley, is hard, mountainous, inaccessible countryside but which contains a number of interesting monasteries and archaeological sites as well as hospitable villages. There are antiquities in Thronos, Monastiraki, and Apodhoulou. In Asomati, where the island's Agricultural School is situated, there is a break in the harsh scenery in the form of lavish vegetation. The little village of Amari itself is very beautiful, and claims to be the local capital despite having fewer than two hundred inhabitants. It contains the oldest frescoes in Crete, which are dated from 1225.

The local tourist authorities also point out that the geological structure of this area means that caves, like the Idi Cave, abound in this district. Exploring caves is not a pastime in which I personally would wish to indulge, but some of them do combine natural beauty with great archaeological and historical interest, although reaching them almost always involves a hard climb. Besides their more academic interest, many of these caves play an important role in Greek mythology – and in this beautiful and mysterious part of Crete, tucked between two vast mountain ranges, it is all too easy to start believing in those legendary figures whom the Greeks of old believed were gods.

9 Chania

There are more romantic spots to choose for an early evening aperitif than beside the jumbled outer harbour of Chania, the second city of Crete. It has an untidy, and even neglected, air about it, with fishing vessels crammed together at the moorings, and crowds of people sitting at the metal topped tables with an *ouzo* or a beer. But it is very Cretan. Swifts wheel and scream overhead, the gossip at the tables ebbs and flows, and the visiting holiday-makers are admired or scorned – privately of course – depending upon their attire. Stay on at the harbourside, and you can eat fresh fish in one of the many *tavernas* for not much more than a few pence.

Chania, however, has another side to it. Situated at the western end of the long north coast of Crete, it is the commercial capital of the Western part of the island, and has a population of about 40,000. It lies on the site of ancient Cydonia. The name Cydonia was found in the Linear-B tablets unearthed at Knossos, and the city's antiquity was confirmed by excavations in the 1960s, which revealed that the site has been inhabited continuously from Neolithic to post-Minoan times. It became, and remained, one of the three most important cities in Crete during the Roman and early Byzantine era, but it probably reached the peak of its importance in 1252, when it was occupied by the Venetians and renamed Canea. The Venetians fortified the city, and the grandeur of its other buildings caused them to christen it 'The Venice of the East'. In 1645 the Turks captured the city, and made it the island capital – a role which it still claims to this day but which is hotly contested by the larger, and more important, Heraklion.

Unfortunately, the battles which have flowed to and fro across Chania – not least during the Second World War – coupled with redevelopment by successive waves of conquerors, have meant that little of the old Venetian structures remain. As a result Chania has, on the surface at any rate, little to show the visitor. But it remains an important communications centre for the western part of the island with both ferry and airline links to Athens on a daily basis. It is growing in popularity as a holiday centre, too, with the development of hotel complexes along the magnificent sandy beaches to the west of the town. There can be little doubt that as the eastern part of the island becomes more crowded with visitors there will be increasing interest in the Chania region and the beaches along the Gulf of Chania.

The original Venetian fortifications, built initially to protect the city from the attentions of the avaricious pirate Barbarossa, were immense – a fifty-yard moat protected the walls and castellated towers. But, apart from the old Kastelli Quarter, little of these fortifications remain. And, as in the case of Heraklion, the town's modern suburbs have spread far beyond the original walled area, although in Chania this development is quite attractive due to the extensive provision of squares and gardens.

At the centre of the town is the covered market, built in the shape of a cross and modelled on the one in Marseilles. The bus station is next to the market, and opposite is the Plateia 1897 (1897 Square). Khatsimikhaili Yiannari Street, which contains a fine minaret, leads to the town's other important square, Plateia 1866, from which there is a good view of the White Mountains. Both squares are just outside the old Venetian walled town, with its untidy streets, and Khalidhon Road leads through the road towards the harbour. Beside the harbour is the Mosque of Hassan Pasha, built in 1645, which is now occupied by the National Tourist Organisation of Greece. In this area parts of the wall are still intact and are worth seeing, as is the Bastion of Schiavo-Lando, which is well preserved.

But rather than a haphazard exploration of Chania it is better to tour, one by one, the five 'quarters' in which the old town is divided: Kastelli in the centre, Evraiki and Tophanas in the west, and Splanzia and Chiones in the east.

The Kastelli Quarter is the name applied to the fortification above the harbour, as well as to the part of the city closest to the harbour. The harbour itself is a very attractive spot, where the people of Chania like to meet and linger over their early evening drinks, or over dinner.

Today the harbour is used only by fishing-boats and yachtsmen, ferry services having been transferred to the port of Souda, a few miles away to the east on the other side of the isthmus of land leading to the skull-shaped Akrotiri Peninsula. Although many of the buildings around the harbour are dilapidated, there are a number of good tavernas serving *mezethes* with your drinks, or even a full-scale meal. The harbour is in two parts. The outer harbour is guarded by its long Venetian mole and Turkish lighthouse, and those who want to walk round to the lighthouse can enter it and climb to the top, from which there is an excellent view of the city. A yacht marina has been constructed in the inner harbour. But it is around the outer harbour that it is best to linger on early or late summer evenings, watching the fishing fleet leaving for their night's work, with white lights bobbing at their mast-heads. The Plaza Hotel, on the quayside, has an external staircase which incorporates an ancient fountain of Venetian or Turkish construction.

Beside the inner harbour is the vaulted Arsenal which was constructed in about 1600. Behind the ruined walls and bastion which survive here stands the Venetian church of Aghios Nikolaos, which was changed by the Turks into the Imperial Mosque of Sultan Ibrahim, when its tower became a minaret, but it was turned back into a Greek Orthodox Church in 1918. The galleried nave has a coffered ceiling. To the east of the church there is a maze of tiny streets which forms the most picturesque corner of the town, and the little church of San Rocco, which bears a Latin inscription dated 1630, is worth visiting.

Stretches of the Inner Wall may be seen between Sfaka Street and Kanevaro Street, but the Kastelli itself was one of the principal casualties of Chania's various battles. Excavations of the Minoan remains here have produced such finds as clay tablets bearing Linear-A inscriptions, and pottery which the Minoans had imported from Cyprus.

The city's Archaeological Museum is imaginatively housed in the Venetian church of San Francesco, in Khalidhon Street close to the harbour, in the Evraiki Quarter. The church itself is crudely constructed. However, the setting, coupled with the careful siting of the exhibits in chronological order, has made this museum one of the most attractive in Crete. Even though it cannot match the glories of Heraklion's exhibits, it contains an interesting collection of vases, terracottas, mosaics, seal stones, jewellery and coins from western Crete. Most notable are the clay *larnakes* (urns), among which there are magnificent polychrome examples from the cemetery of Armenoi. The latter include one illustrated with double axes and bulls.

The museum also contains proto-geometric pottery and a Roman mosaic, Archaic figurines from Axos, and classical bronze mirrors and sculptures. The statue of Aphrodite, from Kydonia, and some marble statues of children from Lissos, are particularly charming.

Outside the walls, the street, Stratigou Tzanakaki, leads from the bus station down past a public park to the historical museum and archives, housed in an area made up of nineteenth-century villas. This contains many rare documents and books from the Byzantine, Venetian and Turkish periods. Ornaments, flags, historical pictures and icons are also included among the exhibits.

Chania's third museum is one which is unique in the island: the Naval Museum, beside the old harbour. This has an interesting collection of items associated with the maritime history of Crete.

In the Tophanas Quarter, the westernmost quarter of the old city, can be found the fine Renieri Gate off Zambeliou Street, with its inscription dating from 1608. Beyond this is a small Venetian chapel, and some old powder magazines. At the end of Theotokopoulou Street is the Venetian church of San Salvatore, which the Turks used as a mosque and which is now a warehouse. This quarter has a strongly Venetian character about it, and it is worth exploring for its wealth of Venetian buildings, even though many of them are in a poor state of preservation.

The church of Aghios Nikolaos, mentioned earlier, is in the Splanzia Quarter, as is the Venetian church of San Rocco. A few streets away, hidden in the narrow lanes, is the church of Aghi Anargyri, a sixteenth-century Greek Orthodox church which was the only one in Chania in which services were allowed during the Venetian and Turkish occupations. It has some very good icons.

The Chiones Quarter is close to the harbour and contains the Arsenal. It is in this area particularly that Chania's chequered history is at its most apparent; the Venetians intended that the harbour should be one of their major trading posts, but never really succeeded in building it up as they had hoped. Many of these jumbles of masonry indicate long-lost building plans, such as the breakwater which they intended should guard the harbour, and the many storage buildings.

In contrast, the Chalepa Quarter is a modern part of Chania, and constitutes a pleasant if hilly suburb. It contains the mansion in which the former Greek Prince George made his home, as well as containing the former Palace of the Governors. It contains many fine villas, some of which served as consulate buildings, and there is also the Convent of the Sisters of St Joseph, an order of French nuns whose influence on the city is still to be seen in the prevalence of French culture. The Church of St Mary Magdelene was built by Prince George's sister, the Grand Duchess Maria, and is in an extraordinary mixture of Gothic and Byzantine styles. The Cretan statesman, Venizelos, also had a house in the Chalepa Quarter, and this is retained by his family. There is a statue of Venizelos nearby, in a small park.

Despite its somewhat care-worn and battered appearance, Chania is a popular city with Cretans, and probably a much more attractive place to live than, say, Heraklion. The big choice of cafes and restaurants, the attractive cruciform market, the squares and gardens, and even a modern swimming-pool, mean that there is every facility for the locals. Facilities for tourists, the *tavernas* excepted, are relatively few; most of the hotel developments are outside the town.

Chania is separated from the huge natural harbour of Souda Bay, now the town's ferry port and an important naval base, by a narrow neck of land leading to the Akrotiri Peninsula – a maze of lanes given over partly to the military and visited principally for its memorial to Venizelos.

There are several good bathing beaches to the west of Chania, between the city and Maleme, which was the scene of some of the heaviest fighting between the Germans and allied forces during the 1941 Battle of Crete.

One of the best, and most under-used, hotels in Crete is on this stretch of coast, the Maleme Beach Hotel, which belongs to the Chandris group. Like so many of the popular new hotels on Crete, this is made up of a series of bungalows around a principal building which contains the restaurant, bars, night club and so on. The bungalows are particularly charming, and there is a huge central swimming-pool as well as the adjacent sandy beach.

The countryside to the south of Chania is dominated by the huge Lefka Ori mountain range, which soars up to over 7,000 feet. The coast road between Chania and Rethymnon wends its way through peaceful farming country, thick with orange groves. The peninsula off to the left of the road, where the countryside is scattered around the little town of Vamos, is not particularly interesting, but at Vryses there is a turning off the main road which leads across the mountains to Chora Sfakion. Vryses itself is a delightful stopping place, shaded by tall plain trees, and has a memorial to the 1898 Cretan rising against the Turks which led to its independence. Then the road climbs through rough unattractive country to Alikampos, which is at the heart of the countryside which is the home of the people of Sfakia, who have become a legend in their own land. The Sfakians – thought to be of original Dorian, or even Saracen, stock – have never been cowed by any of the terror imposed by various occupations of the island, and their ferocity in battle is renowned. Perhaps fortunately for the rest of Crete, however, the Sfakians spend a lot more time fighting one another than they do in fighting other people, for they still believe strongly in the vendetta, and family often takes revenge on family in feuds which last for generations. Despite their ferocity, however, the people of Sfakia also have a majestic courtesy about them. And some of their quaint traditions remain to this day – for example if you wash with a Sfakian he will not pass the soap to you by hand because of a local superstition that this will wash away friendship.

In the middle of the island, below Petres, there are magnificent views of the coast. Then the road drops rapidly down to the tiny south-coast port of Chora Sfakion, which was the site of the dramatic evacuation of more than 10,000 British and Commonwealth troops after the Battle of Crete in 1941.

Today Chora Sfakion is a tiny little port, surrounded by steep hills, which appears to simply doze in the sun. There are a couple of little seafront *tavernas* specializing in sea food and local wines, and the cheap, clean Xenia Hotel. No longer a battleground, it sees nothing more exciting than a few excursion coaches, and the boats returning from excursions to the Gorge of Samaria which is described in the next chapter. The pebble beach is not particularly good for swimming, but it is notable that many Cretans think of it as an ideal resort both for swimming and relaxing.

It is hard to imagine that, four hundred years ago, Chora Sfakion was the largest town on the south coast of Crete, with a population of about 3,000 and – according to local legend – exactly one hundred chapels and churches. Most of the latter, which were built by individuals thankful for their commercial success in the town, have now fallen into disrepair, although several of the churches are intact and can be visited. One of these is the Church of the Holy Apostle, on a hill just above the village, which is the most famous. Several others boast Byzantine frescoes, whilst on the road to Komitadhes, just outside Chora Sfakion, is the Thymniani Panaghia church, which is where the Sfakians held their 'national' assemblies prior to 1821.

Chora Sfakion was once the commercial centre of the Sfakia province and its transition into a tiny holiday resort has been remarkable. It also served, for many years, as a centre for the various revolutionary activities and insurgency in which the Sfakians so loved to indulge. Many caves in the area, which can be visited, are famous in Cretan and Sfakian folklore, the most famous being the Cave of 'John the Clerk' or Cave of Daskaloyiannis, one of Crete's best known revolutionary leaders, which is close to Chora Sfakion and can be reached by sea. 'John the Clerk' led the Cretan uprising against the Turks in 1770, met them to discuss surrender terms, and was seized, tortured and finally horribly killed by the troops who had been given the task of suppressing the revolt.

But an even more emotive spot for Cretans is another popular tourist place, the Venetian fortress known as Frangokastello, or Frankish Castle. This was built in the fourteenth century by the Venetians, with the unsuccessful aim of suppressing the Sfakians. It is a big, square fortress, with four corner towers and is in a good state of preservation.

A road just inland from the coast links Chora Sfakion with Frangokastello. You can take a bus from Chora Sfakion to Patsianos, which is within walking distance of the castle. En route, look out for the village of Komitadhes, where the fourteenth-century church has some very good frescoes.

After the Venetian occupation the Turks also decided to turn the Frangokastello into a military stronghold, and they carried out extensive repairs in the early part of the nineteenth century. But the repairs were of little immediate benefit to them, for in 1828 Cretan revolutionaries under the leadership of Michalis Daliannis seized the castle. A strong Turkish force under the command of Pasha Moustafa was sent to recapture the castle, and the Cretan rebel force, three hundred and eighty-six-strong, was ordered to abandon the building rather than do battle against impossible odds. But Daliannis decided to ignore the order, and he and his men locked themselves inside Frangokastello to await the Turks. There was a long and savage battle, and the defenders and the attackers virtually wiped each other out. Ever since that day the Frangokastello has witnessed a strange phenomenon which still has not been satisfactorily explained.

Every year, on a day in the second fortnight in May, a little before dawn, when the sea is calm and the atmosphere peaceful, a long row of apparently human shadows, dressed in black and carrying bright weapons, walk or ride on horseback across the plain near the castle, as though they were taking part in military exercises. The phenomenon lasts for about ten minutes, and has been witnessed by hundreds of people standing on the castle ramparts. But attempts to approach the mysterious figures have never been successful, and they always vanish without trace. Because they appear in the early morning, the Cretans have named these ghostly shadows the 'Drosoulites', or 'those of the dew'. Scientists say, unconvincingly, that the phenomenon is a reflection, or mirage, of a camel train or military exercises on the adjacent coast of north Africa. But the local people will tell you that the Drosoulites are shadows of Michalis Daliannis and the three hundred and eighty-five Cretan fighting men who died with him on that very spot a century and a half ago. It is an odd little ghost story, and one which has been too frequently witnessed, and too widely documented, to be dismissed out of hand. Perhaps it is the atmosphere of the place. The massive fortress looks imposing enough from the outside, its battlements intact. But inside it is a mere shell. If they linger anywhere, then ghosts could surely linger here.

On a more earthly plane, Frangokastello has a very good beach and three waterside *tavernas* which, besides offering excellent food, have rooms to let. This is one of the more fascinating corners of Crete, and a great place to visit and explore – especially if you happen to be there in the latter half of May.

10 Exploring Western Crete

We were, I suppose, as motley a crowd as it is possible to imagine, who gathered outside the tour offices in Heraklion. We included a couple of English shopgirls in platform-soled shoes, a group of elderly Germans dressed in leather trousers and heavy climbing boots, two youths in shorts and training shoes, and any number of middle-aged couples. But as we clambered aboard a couple of coaches and set off west along the coast road to Chania, we had one aim in common: to walk the full length of the Gorge of Samaria.

The Gorge of Samaria, hidden among the Lefka Ori, or White Mountains, south of Chania, is the longest and most beautiful gorge in Europe – a fourteen-mile crevice slicing its way down to the sea through sheer rock faces which at times tower 2,000 feet above you. It is also extremely narrow in some places, with a minimum width of only 9 feet. Passing, as it does, through one of the wildest and most remote corners of Crete, it has also become a popular excursion in recent years – so however remote it may be, it is never lonely.

But, despite the disadvantages of travelling as part of a large group, it is advisable to walk the Gorge of Samaria as part of an organized excursion. For a start, the gorge is also the bed of a strong mountain stream, and may become impassable after heavy rain, just as it is in the winter and spring when the snows of the White Mountains are melting; but tour guides know the danger signals. Secondly, anyone walking alone and suffering an accident in the gorge could wait many hours before being found. And, thirdly, there is no way out of the gorge except the way you came in – unless you have arranged for a boat to be waiting for you at the tiny village of Aghia Roumeli, at the foot of the gorge. Like several other Cretan villages, Aghia Roumeli has no road at all, and can be approached only from the sea.

The trips to the Gorge, which last two days, start from all over Crete, with the coaches converging on large hotels in and around

Chania for an overnight stop, and then making a start at five o'clock in the morning to drive across the precipitous mountains and the marshy Plain of Omalos to Xyloskalon, where the walk starts.

There is a tourist pavilion at the head of the gorge, and the rocky climb down to the Libyan Sea takes between four and six hours. Fall behind, and you may be fortunate enough to see a golden eagle soaring high above you, or a nimble wild *agrimi* goat leaping among the cliffs – but you may also miss the boat at Aghia Roumeli. 'You must keep together', urged the guide as we started down the steep steps which mark the start of this expedition.

Strictly speaking, I suppose, the walk is only for the fit and the adventurous – although those who are neither often complete it quite comfortably. Officially it is sixteen-and-a-half kilometres (just over ten miles) from end to end, although the twists in the path as it follows the track of the stream undoubtedly brings it up to about fourteen miles. The Gorge is a National Park, and the notice staring you in the face as you begin the walk is suitably stern: 'The disturbance, the stoning, the capture, the wonyding (*sic*), or the murder of any wild animal is forbidden.' You need sensible footwear – the Germans' climbing boots and the shopgirls' platform-soled shoes both being equally unsuitable and, one might suppose, uncomfortable. Don't carry anything if you can help it: by lunchtime it is going to be very hot indeed and you will regret it.

The walk starts with a long, easy descent down through forests of pine and cypress trees. It gets less easy as the steps begin to appear endless. Xyloskalon, however, is 3,500 feet above sea level, and those self-same steps have got to take you down to within a few hundred feet of sea level. After a little while you begin to notice that the steps appear to be carefully arranged so that no two paces are the same length, the ground is getting stonier and more slippery, and your thigh muscles are hurting.

The youths in training shoes and shorts went past at a run. The girls in platform-soled shoes clutched at one another and giggled a lot. The German party strode out manfully, swinging heavy sticks and with hefty rucksacks on their backs. An elderly lady began to wish that she had never come, and said so at frequent intervals.

After a while the path reaches the level of the stream, and the steps come to an end. Briefly, the Gorge widens out – affording magnificent views across to Lefka Ori, where the early morning sun is catching the peaks which, if it is still early summer, may yet have snow on them. Behind you a couple of 6,000 foot peaks rise sheer from the path. The track itself is distinct and well surfaced on this stretch – but already your legs and feet ache.

It is a good two hours, however, before you see ahead of you the halfway point: the village of Samaria. It comes almost as a disappointment to find that the village is deserted, although there is water there. But there are some shadowy entrepreneurs lurking among the trees surrounding the tumble-down buildings: enterprising locals waiting with donkeys to rescue the faint-hearted. If by chance they are not there, rumour has it that you can telephone an SOS using a receiver hidden in a tree – but either way the rescue squad is important. It is after Samaria that the going really gets hard, and it is about now, too, that the day is really warming up. What is more, people totally unsuited to the walk – like our elderly lady – frequently attempt it even though they could never hope to complete it. Our elderly lady was duly evacuated – at a price. And the three German hikers, who had been slowing perceptibly, turning very red, and perspiring freely, were seen to remain behind as we all set off again, and to engage the donkey drivers in animated conversations.

For a little while the walk continues through lush vegetation – wild sage and thyme scenting the air, wild orchids and iris lending splashes of colour. But those massive rock walls are closing in on you, and slowly they shut out the sunlight. And the path is getting harder, too – for now you often have to clamber from rock to rock on the bed of the stream itself. You can stop and drink the water from the stream, which is perfectly clean, extremely refreshing, and in fact supplies water to the settlements at the bottom of the Gorge. But they prefer it if you do not wash your feet in their drinking water, and any impromptu bathers can expect a torrent of abuse from the guide.

There are a couple of points at which the towering cliffs on either side of the path close in until they almost touch one another, giving an oddly claustrophobic effect. At the narrowest point the gap narrows to less than nine feet and the rock walls – known at this spot as 'the iron gates' – seem about to crush you. But there is nowhere, as some guide books claim, where a man can stand and touch the cliffs on either side of him. In these narrow stretches of the Gorge the path becomes non-existent, and walkers have then to hop from rock to rock.

Eventually walkers emerge at the remote village of Aghia Roumeli, an inhospitable little spot where the walk is still not complete. You still have to tramp across a couple of miles of scorching shingle to the beach – where there are a couple of all-too-welcome *tavernas* waiting with long, cool drinks, and a beach where you can hurl yourself thankfully into the sea.

We found the young men in shorts and running shoes already enjoying their lunch, having taken only three hours to cover the entire length of the Gorge. The shopgirls were close behind them – with their platform-soled shoes dangling from their hands and as handsome a collection of cuts and blisters on their feet as one could ever imagine. But at least they had made it. Everyone else, excepting the Samaria evacuees, made it too – the stragglers taking no more than five hours for the walk. And the last to arrive, to a derisive round of cheering, were the German hikers – riding shamefacedly on hired donkeys.

Because we were on an organized group excursion, a large fishing boat, or *caique*, was waiting to transfer us to Chora Sfakion. But solo walkers have to make an important decision when they reach Aghia Roumeli. They can telephone Chora Sfakion and try to hire a *caique*, perhaps taking a look at the site of ancient Tarrha, on the outskirts of Aghia Roumeli, while they wait for the boat to arrive. They can take the coastal path – another fourteen mile walk – to Chora Sfakion, passing en route the Chapel of St Paul built on a spot where the apostle is said to have come ashore on Crete. Or they can begin the long, hard climb back up the Gorge. The latter, likely to take about eight hours, is not recommended.

As has been mentioned earlier, there are a number of similar, but much smaller gorges along Crete's south coast – none of them as accessible as the Gorge of Samaria, and none as dramatic, but several of them more beautiful. There are no coach loads of tourists walking these gorges, and no harrying guides. But I found the Samaria walk, though tiring, an exciting and truly memorable experience which I would not want to trade for the smaller gorges which the Cretans themselves prefer. Walking the Gorge of Samaria is an emotional experience, bringing one closer to the wild, beautiful and dramatic countryside. And those who have not done it cannot claim to know Crete.

There are a number of other interesting places to explore in western Crete, but a car is essential, for transport in this area is related entirely to the needs of the villages. It is only fair to add that this is a section of the island which is seldom visited by tourists, and the roads can be very bad. Secondary roads in Crete are not necessarily tarred. They are often hardbacked roads with gravel surfaces, particularly in the south and west of the island. They may be slightly eroded, or well pitted with potholes, and they can be dusty in summer and slippery in winter. But at least they are solid. Roads leading to the more isolated places are often unpaved, but are treated with gravel, which does help.

Most towns and villages have petrol stations, and these are well signposted with the familiar road sign depicting a fuel pump. In an emergency, the grocers' shops in most small villages also sell small quantities of petrol (ask for *benzini*). Most places also have repair facilities, although spares may be hard to find outside the main towns. The repairs themselves may look very crude if you stop to watch the work being done, but do not worry. The Greeks share with the Arabs a genius for improvisation when it comes to getting a vehicle back on the road. In case of real difficulty, ask for the tourist police or call in at any police station and explain that you are a visitor.

There is, incidentally, an island speed limit of 30 k.p.h. in towns and other built-up areas. Main roads outside built-up areas are derestricted, except where marked. But, despite the habits of local drivers which may suggest otherwise, Crete is not an island in which it pays to drive at any speed. Quite apart from the fact that by driving fast you will miss the scenery, the mountains mean that most roads are narrow and twist and turn quite alarmingly and, in some places, are badly signposted. The reverse cambers and precipitous bends are another hazard to bear in mind. And remember that, in the towns and villages, pedestrians have right of way. That is why Cretans often amble along quite happily in the middle of the road, oblivious of any apparent danger. Combine this habit with the occasional unlit vehicle at night and the slow-moving flocks of sheep and goats which use some country roads in the daytime, and one can see that Crete is an island in which the car driver needs both a great deal of care and patience.

On the north coast of the island, beyond Maleme, two great peninsulas, Rodopos and Gramvousa, jut into the sea. But there are no real roads on either of the peninsulas, only tracks, and there is little point in visiting either of them unless you wish to see the site of the Doric town of Diktyna, on Rodopos.

Like Lato, in the east, Diktyna is an emotive spot – ruins set amid splendid isolation. Its second-century BC temple, the Sanctuary of Artemis Diktyna, dominated the town, and was built on the site of two earlier temples. The ruins are still worth exploring, but reaching them is hard going. Diktyna, is in the north-east corner of the Rodopos peninsula, and getting there involves turning off the main road to Kolimvari and Afrata, after which you must walk for several hours. Perhaps a better route is by *caique* from Kolimvari – local fishermen will happily make the excursion, but at a price.

Between the Rodopos and Gramvousa peninsulas, on the Kissamou Gulf, is the little town of Kastelli – a straggle of buildings set behind a fine beach. It stands on the site of ancient Kissamos, and Kastelli itself was a thriving Venetian town. Today it tends more towards sleepiness than industry, although there is plenty of wine-growing and farming round about. The museum in Kastelli contains local finds, but gaining access to the museum can be a major problem in itself if the custodian is not around. There is a whole jumble of villages around this area, some of them given over to forestry rather than farming. Beyond Kastelli the road turns south for Platanos, where some proto-geometric pottery has been found, and a side road leads down to a lovely sandy beach beneath shady olive groves.

Another road to cross the western part of Crete runs from Maleme to Kandanos, a major town in this area until the Germans destroyed it in heavy fighting in this area in 1941, and the remote little south coast resort of Paleochora, which was fortified by the Venetians and has a large beach backed by trees. Paleochora has one ungraded hotel, plenty of private rooms to let, and not a few *tavernas*. This is one of the undiscovered corners of Crete, and an attractive destination for those who can make the pilgrimage across the mountains by car or infrequent bus.

There are other beauty spots, and island oddities, in this region – hard to find, yet worth the finding. I like the little church just outside Kouneni, with its extraordinary thirteenth-century frescoes. They are extraordinary because, when the ceiling fell in, the villagers repaired it themselves – but found the jigsaw too hard for them, and put many of the pieces back in the wrong places with quite memorable (yet beautiful, rather than funny) results. The original sketches in the apse make an interesting comparison with the paintings themselves, and show much of the manner in which the old Cretan masters worked. I like, too, Polyrrhenia, near Kastelli, sweetly scented in spring and early summer by the herbs which grow there. Polyrrhenia means 'city of many flocks' – but city of many spices might have been a better name.

Then there are the panoramic coastal views of Gramvousa from the village of Phalasarna, near Platanos. And the harbour of ancient Phalasarna, now a hundred and fifty yards inland and twenty-eight feet above sea level because of the rapid movement of the land in this corner of the island.

And there are more good frescoes in three villages close to Kandanos: Aniskari, Kavalariana and Drys. Look out especially for the fourteenth-century fresco of the Empty Tomb at the Panaghia church in Aniskari, and those by the master, Pagomenos, at Kavalariana.

In a way, it is hard to know what to make of the western part of Crete. It is full of villages, yet none of them is of sufficient beauty or interest to have yet found a real place on the tourist map. And even where there is something interesting to see, all too often it seems to have been damaged or destroyed by anything from enemy action to an act of God. There are any number of prospective archaeological sites too – but the accent is on the word prospective, for few of them have been properly excavated yet. The roads are usually bad, and much of the countryside is harsh.

Perhaps, after all, one should abandon the car and walk. Or even take the boat from Kastelli out to the little island of Agri Gramvousa, at the tip of the Gramvousa Peninsula, where the Venetians built the last of their protective string of forts around the island and its leading natural harbours.

Perhaps this is truly the forgotten corner of Crete. There are no tourist developments here. Even Chania is an hour or more away by car, and none of the more dubious products of tourist development have reached the villages, where the island folk still tend their gardens, smallholdings and olive groves, look after their goats, and sit outside the *taverna* of an evening to talk over the events of a day which is always different, yet always the same. Not that the islanders mind that. In fact, I suspect they prefer it that way.

11 Food and Shopping

The menus in many popular Cretan holiday resorts are often of the new, international variety. Holidaymakers, a few restaurants seem to have decided, will never have the courage to adopt the Greek tradition and go into the kitchen to inspect the food as it is being prepared and cooked, so they take advantage of a comprehensive mass-produced menu with prices written against those dishes which are 'on'. But that should not be taken as being too indicative of the state of Greek cooking. A few years ago it was common to read and hear quite savage attacks on the awfulness of Greek food, with travel experts advising holidaymakers to carry with them every medicament short of a stomach pump. It is doubtful whether these criticism were ever justified, and they are certainly not true today. Admittedly many Greek dishes are an acquired taste, and sometimes the only *taverna* to be found in some very remote parts of Crete may be, to say the least, somewhat basic. A diet of stale, oily meat and *retsina*, the resinated wine so beloved by Greeks, will play havoc with the hardiest constitution; but no doubt a Cretan would be equally upset by an elderly pork pie and some stewed tea in a grubby roadside cafe in England. Eat wisely in Crete, choosing from local and traditional Greek dishes, and you will eat well. Indeed, a meal will quickly become the prolonged pleasure that it is to almost every Cretan.

The first secret of any Cretan meal is not to be in a rush – because even if you are, the waiters won't be. Office hours throughout Greece are broken by a long siesta in the afternoon, especially during the summer months, so even a light lunch need not be a hurried affair. Businessmen work late, then join their friends or family for what is often the social highlight of the day: dinner. Country folk do likewise, often after a picnic lunch in the fields. And whether they are eating at home, or out in a restaurant or *taverna*, the Greeks like to sit long over their aperitifs (usually aniseed-flavoured *ouzo*, which turns cloudy when you add water or ice and is surprisingly strong, or else the fiery Cretan spirit *raki*) and then chat between courses. The men may even stand up and perform a lonely *syrtaki* dance to the music of the *bouzouki* when the mood takes them. It is bad manners to applaud such dancing, for the man dancing alone is considered to be performing a private act of communion with himself – but tourists usually clap and will be forgiven for their ignorance.

At a party, or feast, the usual system is for the waiters to bring course after course to the table and for people to take whatever they want; at such meals appetites are always exhausted long before the menu is. In some very remote areas of Crete the old eastern European and Middle Eastern custom of eating from a communal pot still survives, although tourists are unlikely to come across it. What holidaymakers may find when eating with Cretans, however, is that they are offered a piece of choice meat or fruit from their companion's plate in the middle of the meal – a complimentary gesture that should not be refused. Equally, it is dangerous to slip into the habit of leaving the choice bit on your own plate until last – for your neighbour may well reach across and help himself!

But these idiosyncracies are rare. Usually you will have to contend with nothing more hazardous than a menu which is in Greek and which may, therefore, be totally unintelligible to you, or with the habit – widely practised throughout Greece – where *taverna* customers walk into the kitchen to choose the main course. It is important to emphasize that no-one will be surprised by such an act in Crete (indeed, the *taverna*-owner may well insist upon it), and the state of the kitchen will do much to ease any remaining qualms you may have about Greek food. Every *taverna* kitchen that I have ever seen has been spotless, even if it was small, hot and overcrowded.

If you want to be adventurous with your choice of food, then a peep into the kitchen will certainly aid your choice. But if not – what should you choose?

Two very safe choices are *souvlaki* or *kebab*, which is meat, usually lamb, grilled on a spit, and *moussaka*, a delicious pie containing minced meat and aubergine. Both are always made with fresh meat. A side salad, or *salata*, is usually ordered too, and this is an impressive affair of huge tomatoes, peppers, liberal quantities of onion, and sprinkled with olives. *Feta*, a hard, crumbly, goat's cheese, which is dipped in olive oil and the taste of which typifies Cretan food, is often served with the salad. Before the main course there are snacks known as *mezethes* – a sort of hors d'oeuvre – or very tasty *taramosa-*

lata, a creamy paste made of fish roes and often eaten with hot *pitta* bread.

On an island like Crete, fish dishes are naturally common, despite claims that the fishing is poor (the absence of algae, on which fish feed, is said to account for the remarkable shade of blue of the water). Pride of place must go the red mullet, or *barbounia*, which is grilled and usually eaten whole – it is absolutely delicious, and a complete meal in itself. Sea bream (*lithinria*) is good also, and visitors should ensure that they do not leave the island without tasting *kalamarakia* (crispy fried pieces of young squid), shellfish, or the sort of *pilaff* made by the islanders of shrimps and prawns.

Other Greek favourites are *dolmades*, vine leaves stuffed with meat and rice and served hot or cold; *avgolemono*, a clear, lemon-flavoured chicken soup; and *youvarlakia*, boiled meat-balls with rice.

A speciality of the island is small cheese pies called *tyropitta* – eaten when they are freshly made and still hot. The hard *feta* goat's cheese, found all over the island, is part of the staple diet and can be recommended. So also is *paximathi*, the dry bread of the island which looks and tastes like a rusk. There is fruit to follow every meal, although your Cretan companions may well choose sticky sweets or cakes instead.

Popular sweets include *baclava*, which is pastry in layers with honey and nuts in between; *kataifi*, again made of sweetened nuts but this time between wheat which has been shredded; and *galaktoboureko* pastries filled with vanilla custard. Many places on the island also make their own yoghurt.

The water is good on Crete, and can be drunk anywhere. But if you are suspicious, a number of mineral-waters are available. Beer is more expensive than wine and, although standards are changing fast, not all brands are good. If you need a beer after a day in the sun, imported *Amstel* is pleasant – although the Greek *Fix* beer can now be found on draught and that, too, is good.

With many areas now producing their own wines, the choice can be bewildering in the best restaurants and non-existent in small country *tavernas* – but Greek wines are, as a general rule, pleasantly light if somewhat stronger than most of their European counterparts. In towns, and in most major hotels, mainland wines such as *Demestica*, from the Peloponnese, and the fuller-bodied *Naoussa* red wine from Macedonia, are available. In the villages you are more likely to get local wines, such as *Minos, Gortys, Kastelli* and *Kissamos*, while in the more out-of-the-way spots the choice is limited to the produce of the local vineyards which is designated simply by colour: *aspro* (white), *mavro* or *kokkino* (red). Many Cretan wines are flavoured with resin to help them to travel, and this *retsina* is one of the distinctive tastes of Greece – although it is not a taste to which every visitor takes immediately. Cretan *retsinas*, such as *Minos*, are less heavily resinated than their mainland counterparts, and can be sampled without too much trepidation. If you are still unsure, ask the advice of the restauranteur or the *taverna*-owner – he will be pleased to recommend a brand without too much resin.

Provided that you allow for the home-made taste (which is, after all, to be expected, for that is what many of these wines are), I have yet to find an undrinkable, or even unpleasant, wine in Crete – although I am assured that they exist. The same cannot always be said for the local brandies. Brandy drinkers should stick to *Metaxa*, and the seven-star *Gold Label Metaxa* at that, although even this is rough compared with its Western European counterparts. Although, like *retsina*, the raw and unflavoured *raki* is an acquired taste, it is preferred as a nightcap by many holidaymakers on the island – and it is certainly strong enough to ensure that you sleep soundly.

Apart from the food, the great attraction of Cretan *tavernas*, as well as some restaurants, is that they are also places of entertainment. There may be a resident band or a singer if you are in a top-class hotel; in less sophisticated parts you may simply find a *bouzouki* player, or even a waiter who every now and again stops serving and sings a song or two instead. And if there is no live entertainment, you may well find that the proprietor has made the best of a bad job and installed a jukebox. Fortunately this is still rare in Crete, but if it is the case don't be put off; the records will all be Greek. Whether they are dining inside or out in the open air, Greeks love a lot of noise.

Tavernas also have one other great factor in their favour: they will never turn you away. High in the Cretan mountains, one day, I stopped for a beer in a small village, and the *taverna* owner discovered to his embarrassment that he had run out of beer. A child was sent running to borrow a couple of bottles from a local householder, and meanwhile, to compensate for my brief wait, there was thick Greek coffee, served in tiny cups that seem to be half full of sediment. This coffee is another acquired taste but, especially if washed down with a glass of water, it can be as refreshing as any drink on the island. Remember, though, to order it medium-sweet, or *metrio* – the Greeks have a far sweeter tooth than we do. For the faint-hearted, instant coffee is available in most parts of the island.

Shopping for souvenirs in Crete is an adventure in itself. Of course you will want at least one set of *kombolia*, the brightly-coloured worry beads with which Greeks play interminably, and perhaps a memento or two of Knossos. Every souvenir shop has these, but prices vary from place to place and – perhaps surprisingly – it is often best to do all one's shopping in the main centres, such as Heraklion, Aghios Nikolaos, Chania or Rethymnon. Some places will let you bargain over prices, and this is almost mandatory in the street markets; but more and more shops have set prices and an 'offer' from you will result only in your getting an excellent view of the shop assistant's back.

In Heraklion, look out for locally-made jewellery, which is very attractive and may be considered cheap; embroidered dresses, which are perfect for a summer's evening; and leather goods, especially shoes. Shoes in the better shops are very fashionable, and a third of the price that they would be at home. You can also get very basic but comfortable leather sandals made to measure for you all over the island – and even in Aghios Nikolaos these work out at only a couple of pounds or so per pair.

Sponges are a popular buy in Crete, although they are not particularly cheap. Pottery is also much sought after, although getting it home safely may present problems. But don't bother with what look like antiques or classical pieces of Greek art. Quite apart from the fact that exporting antiquities without a licence is forbidden, the Cretans have developed the faking of antiques – and particularly weapons – into an art. There is the occasional medium-priced icon to be found, although this is more likely on the Greek mainland. Modern reproductions are often convincing and attractive, but occasionally quite bad.

In the resorts, boutiques are beginning to flourish, but – although the goods they offer are remarkably attractive – they are usually expensive by Cretan standards. The same applies to the shopping arcades which are just beginning to sprout in the major tourist hotels – a regrettable American and western European practice that is only now spreading to Crete. These shops are excellent for browsing through and for purchasing newspapers, toilet requisites and other minor items, but like airport shops they are run on a concessionary basis and prices may be inflated. I have always found that I can do better outside the hotel when making anything but a minor purchase.

Shopping hours vary according to the season. In most places the shops open from 8.00 am until at least 7.30 pm in summer, but they close at 1.00 pm for a three-hour siesta. Early closing days are Wednesday and Saturday. In the principal resorts, however, many shops remain open long into the evening, which is the time when they are busiest with shoppers who have been on excursions, or on the beach, all day. In the large towns, chemists work a twenty-four hour rota as in Britain, and a similar service is offered by the principal hotels.

For minor purchases, small kiosks in the main squares of the towns are ideal: they sell cigarettes, sweets, postcards, proprietary brands of medicine, newspapers – everything that they can cram into their windows. You can make local telephone calls from these kiosks, too. They often stay open very late at night, but hours vary according to the proprietor's whim.

12 Sports and Activities

Although Crete cannot be described as a major sporting venue, it does have the facilities for most sports and outdoor pastimes – albeit somewhat basic at times. These facilities are not always obvious at first; you have to go and look for them. But they are there, and they are all the more enjoyable because so few people know about them.

Take the waters of the Aegean, to the north of Crete, for example. These are famous sailing waters, and Crete is on the itinerary of any week-long voyage from Piraeus, the port of Athens. But it is just as enjoyable to start a sailing holiday in Crete, or to hire a *caique* in Heraklion harbour and sail north or north-east towards some of the justly famous, and very beautiful, Aegean islands. Alternatively, there are a number of boat excursions from the major resort areas on Crete to the minor islands just offshore; these are described in the relevant chapters in this book.

The main sailing centres in Crete are Heraklion and Aghios Nikolaos. From both of these, the islands of Milos, Karpathos and the lovely Santorini are within easy reach – a day's sailing. Santorini, a major key to the Minoan mystery, tends to be overcrowded with trippers these days, but its dramatic setting, and the long climb on the back of a donkey or mule from the harbour up to the principal town of Fira, make the trip well worthwhile. Milos, and Karpathos in particular, are less crowded – and the latter is one of the most beautiful islands in the Aegean. From Karpathos it is only a short crossing to Rhodes, so Crete can be used as the starting and finishing point for a sailing tour of the southern Aegean.

Hiring a yacht to sail yourself is not expensive in Crete, but the hire of a crewed vessel can become a costly business. The largest vessels can cost up to £1,000 a day – but for that you get a mini-liner with every imaginable luxury. Hiring a *caique*, accommodating from four to ten passengers, costs up to one hundred pounds a day, but the boat comes complete with a crew who are expert in these waters.

And that is no mean consideration, for the Aegean – particularly in the autumn – can prove to be a surprisingly rough and dangerous sea even though, when sailing in it, you are never long out of sight of land.

The most attractive yacht sailing is in the Gulf of Mirabello, off Aghios Nikolaos. There are hiring facilities in the town itself, but many of the large hotels in this area also hire out their own one- or two-person dinghies and there are a number of interesting excursions to be made in these protected waters. There is also quite good sailing at the other end of the island, around Chania, although this is less popular and less well known at present.

The other aquatic sports for which Crete is known are, of course, swimming, water-skiing and skin-diving. The swimming is superb almost everywhere, and individual beaches have already been described. But it is always important to look out for local currents, and to seek advice before swimming far from the shore. There are no lifeguards on Cretan beaches and the waters can be tricky. It is safest to swim from the beaches which are controlled or overlooked by the major hotels, or from the public beaches adjacent to the main towns which have full facilities.

Skin-diving and scuba-diving are increasingly popular in Crete, where the waters are ideal – particularly in and around the Gulf of Mirabello. But once again caution is essential. The diver who is experienced and fit, however, need have no fears. And besides the delights of underwater flora and fauna, there are several places where submerged remains may be examined. These include Arvi, Elounda, Matala and Rethymnon. Skin-diving equipment is available for sale or hire in Heraklion and Chania, and more recently in Aghios Nikolaos. But scuba-divers will have to take their equipment with them to the island.

The use of compressed air harpoons and spears in Cretan waters is frowned upon by the authorities, and divers would be well advised not to indulge in this sport unless they have the permission of the local harbour-master. Harbour-masters in Crete have much more extensive powers than they do in Britain, and they hold sway over both their local port and the adjacent coastline. But they are approachable and friendly, and their advice should be heeded as well as sought. There are no restrictions on any other kind of fishing, although anglers may find the island's waters distinctly unproductive. If you must fish, it is best to approach the local fishermen who will often take visitors out on their night fishing trips – an attractive and romantic expedition if the sea is not rough. Night fishing fleets, with their distinctive lanterns bobbing at the masthead of each vessel, operate from Chania, Rethymnon, Aghios Nikolaos, Sitia and Ierapetra, among others.

It is also possible to hunt on Crete, although this is seldom done by the holiday-maker. The island has quite a lot of small game, including rabbits, hares, partridges, woodcock and ducks. You need a licence, and the tourist police in Heraklion can advise on this as well as helping the visitor to find ways around the official regulation that such licences cannot normally be granted to someone who has not been resident on the island for six months or more. It is important to note that the wild *agrimi* goat, which is indigenous to Crete, is a protected animal, and anyone shooting one of these animals is subject to heavy penalties.

Water-skiing, newly popular on Crete, is available at a number of major hotels, including the Minos Beach and the Elounda Beach hotels at Aghios Nikolaos, the Blue Sea Hotel at Stalis, and the Creta Beach and the Knossos Beach hotels near Heraklion. The sport is relatively inexpensive for guests at these hotels, but visitors would be well advised to put their names down early, as there is often a queue. The major hotels are also the only place where one is likely to find tennis courts – but these are often floodlit so it is not necessary to play in the heat of the day.

After sunbathing and swimming, the most popular outdoor activities on Crete are probably walking, climbing, and riding. But if you tend to indulge in the latter, do not expect to find any well cared for stables and thoroughbred horses. Your mount will be at best a mule, and possibly only a lowly donkey. But don't despair, these game little animals are not only fun to ride, they are also the only way it is possible – even today – to reach some of the remoter corners of the island. They are particularly well suited to the mountainous centre of the island, and it is possible to hire a donkey, and a guide too, in almost any village. Hire charges are ridiculously low, and in country areas you can haggle. Many visitors from northern Europe are reluctant to ride a donkey – the beasts look too small, and too fragile, to carry one over long distances. (Sadly, they are often treated with casual indifference, and even apparent cruelty, by their owners – who will only laugh if you protest, and may even tell you the hoary old story that a donkey contains the soul of a person who has been sentenced to purgatory, and that they therefore deserve all that they get!) But they are tough little beasts, and quite used to carrying heavy burdens. They are also surprisingly comfortable to ride, and if one intends to make a one or two day excursion into the mountains they are to be recommended, and will be far more footsure than a mule.

In the unlikely event of a visitor being unable to hire a donkey, it is worth considering buying one. There is a ready market for donkeys in Crete, and at the end of your excursion you will almost certainly be able to sell it back to its original owner, or to another villager, for as much as you paid for it. The Cretans will admire your business sense, and you will have enjoyed a free excursion. But Cretans can drive a hard bargain too – and anyone you are trying to sell a donkey to will be only too well aware that you have a plane to catch, and that the beast will be of little use to you at Heraklion airport.

The most popular walks in Crete are those down the Gorge of Samaria, and up to the Dictaean Cave. These have already been described, but it should be emphasized that there is plenty of fine walking in the Cretan mountains, and hikers will find that there are plenty of villages along the route which will be only too happy to provide food and lodgings. This is an extremely cheap way to get around Crete, if only because prices in the mountain villages are ridiculously low, and an evening meal and bed for the night can still leave one with change from two pounds. But the country is hard, and there is no point in pretending otherwise. You need to be an experienced walker and, most importantly, you need to be properly shod. There is good climbing on the island too, but the vagaries of the weather, with snow remaining on the peaks until well into the summer, mean that this aspect of the island is still one which has been little explored. Both climbers and walkers will be rewarded with some magnificent views, and with an insight into Crete which few visitors normally experience.

Botanists and ornithologists will also find Crete much to their liking, and a very rewarding place in which to explore. The island has an unusual variety of flowers, plants and trees, said to number well over 1,500 with at least 100 of them peculiar to the island. Because the island has such a variety of climates (it can still be freezing up in the mountains, while the coastline is simmering in a spring heat wave), the island has a little of everything. The quince is said to have originated on Crete, and the wild herb dittany, a member of the mint family similar to wild marjoram, is distinctive to the island. It is found growing throughout the island, particularly in mountain areas, and is used by the Cretans as a flavouring for many of their dishes. It is also said to have therapeutic qualities for women in childbirth.

Rumour has it that the Cretan mountain dwellers wear high boots for fear of snakes. But, like Ireland, the island has no snakes – they are reputed to have been expelled by St Titus. Rather, the boots are worn because many of the wild plants and shrubs growing in the hills are unpleasantly spiked. The fauna of the island is not particularly distinctive – and remarkably similar to the British Isles. The fiercest animal that you are likely to meet is a wildcat, and these are rarely seen. Shrews, mice, rats, rabbits, hares, martens, weasels, badgers, hedgehogs and bats are far more often seen. The bird life is too extensive to detail; because the island is a major stopping point for many migrating varieties, it is possible to see almost anything on Crete. But look out especially for the golden eagle, which patrols the skies over the rocky gorges of the south coast.

Pride of place among the fauna goes, of course, to the wild *agrimi* goat, mentioned at regular intervals throughout this book.

On a less esoteric level, the night life of Crete – a major preoccupation with holidaymakers – can be disappointing. The Cretans themselves are content with an early evening drink, an informal stroll along the seafront or through the main street of their village or town, and a long, lingering evening meal. But Heraklion, the north coast resorts and Aghios Nikolaos have quickly learnt to cater for their visitors' needs by introducing discos and local shows which feature dancers in national costume. The discos can be lively, particularly in and around Aghios Nikolaos. But the same cannot be said for the shows, which personal experience suggests are cobbled together by local entrepreneurs with little or no knowledge of, or interest in, the island's traditions. I have seen such shows which included dancing from all over Greece – although the audience were left with the impression that they were all peculiar to Crete. It is best to seek local advice before seeing one of these shows; the real thing is available, but all too rarely.

Heraklion, Chania and Rethymnon have night clubs, featuring western music and dancing. And there are also a few cinemas which should not be ignored: the films which they show are very often in English, with Greek sub-titles, and thus can be enjoyed by British and North American visitors. The only problem is that the cinemas tend to be stuffy; Crete has not yet caught on to the pleasant habit of introducing open-air cinemas, which are now to be found all over the Greek mainland. One exception to this is Aghios Nikolaos.

The mysteries of Greek food, and particularly Cretan food, have already been explored, but one point does bear making here, and that is the rule of Cretan hospitality which applies to the payment for a meal. If you happen to be dining with a Cretan, it is most unlikely that you will be allowed to pay. The host will quietly pay for the meal before it is officially over, and on no account should one attempt to argue with this, or – horror of horrors – try to organize a whip-round among one's fellow guests. The western European habit of 'going Dutch' is considered to be the height of rudeness in Crete. If you are the host at a meal it is possible that one or other of the Cretans among your guests will attempt to pay the bill before you do, because he still considers you to be a guest on his island. To avoid giving any offence, it is best to try to pay the bill as un-ostentatiously as possible a little before the end of the meal; the restaurant or *taverna* owner will then politely inform anyone else who tries to pay that the bill has already been settled. Much the same rules apply to the buying of rounds of drinks.

For those content to spend their days sitting in the sun, British newspapers and the European editions of American newspapers, usually a day old, are available in all the main towns and at the principal hotels – although they are universally expensive. A great variety of paperback books, in English, is also widely available.

Medical facilities on the island are surprisingly extensive, and a doctor can always be found quickly and easily. Visitors have to pay for medical and dental treatment, so it is wise to take out health insurance before going on holiday to Crete. Language is seldom a problem as most doctors have been trained outside Greece and speak at least one major European language. Chemist's shops, which are marked with a red cross, can be found in all the main towns and many villages, and carry a large stock of proprietary medicines as well as dispensing prescriptions. But visitors hiking or riding in the hills, or going off to the more remote corners of the island, would still be well advised to carry a first-aid kit.

Banks have branches in all the main towns, and these are open from 9.00 am to 1.00 pm. But Greek banks are usually very crowded, and the service can be tortuously slow – a factor which is encouraged by the need to see both a bank clerk and a cashier before completing even the simplest operation, such as cashing a traveller's cheque. It is easiest to cash traveller's cheques at the larger hotels, where you may get a very slightly poorer rate but where the service will be much faster, or even in the many shops which will quite happily accept, and even give change for, traveller's cheques or foreign currency. Exchange rates vary from day to day, but in the case of a small village you may often find that a shopkeeper invents his own exchange rate. Don't reject this out of hand – quite often the visitor seems to benefit from this arrangement.

Greece uses the standard metric weights and measures, and you buy fruit, for example, in kilos. The electricity supply on the island is not particularly reliable, although strenuous efforts are being made to improve this, and it is still advisable to take dual-voltage razors or hair-dryers on a trip to Crete. There can still be prolonged interruptions to supplies at times – although many of the larger hotels have now made their own arrangements and escape this hazard.

The post to and from places outside Greece is equally hazardous, and may be subjected to considerable delays. Even mail to and from places within Greece takes two or three days. So you should expect to get home before your holiday postcards, and should merely be pleasantly surprised if this does not prove to be the case.

* * *

But a chapter on 'Sports and Activities' ends up a book on an island whose inhabitants are characterized, in fact, by their very relaxed inactivity. And their lassitude, one discovers, is not only typical of Crete, but it can be catching. Crete ensures that the excesses caused by or for tourists are kept within reasonable bounds. It does this by its geography, and by the character of its people.

Crete's few real resort areas have, with one or two noteworthy exceptions, always sprung up where they did no harm to anybody. Its archaeological sites never really get overcrowded – there are too many of them. And its roads never get too overcrowded either – for the most part they are too rough. There is no price-cutting in the tourist shops – indeed, quite the opposite is true. And when you arrive in the island, or when you leave, Greek officialdom is laborious and unhurried in clearing your path. In short, Crete accepts and welcomes its visitors – but it does so on its own terms.

And that is just as it should be. For Crete is an island to savour: a place where you learn a little, leave, and then return to learn more.

It is an island of dreams; an island where, perhaps more than anywhere else, Greece lives up to all its expectations; an island where you can explore when the mood takes you, but where you will probably spend most of your time lying in the sun, making great plans, but doing practically nothing.

Index

A
Abbot Gabriel 97
Acropole Hotel 93
Aegean, 18, 20, 38, 135
Afrata 117
Agamemnon, King 22
Aghia Anargyri, Church of 107
Aghia Deka 90
Aghia Galini 93
Aghia Roumeli 112, 113, 114, 115
Aghia Triada 37, 44, 90, 92, 93
Aghia Varvara 90
Aghios Ioannis 88
Aghios Nicolaos 13, 16, 48, 50, 53, 54, 58, 61, 63, 85, 123, 125, 126, 127, 129, 130
   museum 57
Agri Gramvousa 118
agrimi goat 49, 99, 113, 129
Ahelis, Antonios 98
Akrotiri Peninsula 106, 108
Akti Zeus Hotel 94
Albania 27
Alexander the Great 23
Alexandria 23
Alexiou, Stylianos 35, 45
Alikampos 109
Amari Valley 102
Amnisos 50
Amos 21
Anapodiaris Valley 90
Aniskari 118
Ano Vianos 89, 90
Anoyia 94, 95
Apodhoulou 102
Argonauts, the 18
Argyroupolis 100
Arimondi, Alvise 97
Aristotle 23

Arkadi Monastery 96
Armenoi 106
Arvari 90
Arvi 126
Ashmolean Museum 34
Asia Minor 38
Asomati 102
Asterousia Mountains 90
Astir Palace Hotel, Elounda 59
Athens 22, 49, 123, 125
Atlantis 21, 22
Attica 21
Augustus, Emperor 24
Axos 107

B
Babylon 23
banks 130, 131
Barbarossa 83, 105
barbounia (red mullet) 121
Belvedere Hotel 51
Bethlehem 24
Blue Sea Hotel 50, 127
botany 128
Botticelli 17
British School, Athens 35
Byzantine 39, 100, 101, 102
Byzantium 24, 25, 101
buses 31, 32

C
camping 50, 100
Candia Beach Hotel 50
Ceram, C.W. 34
Chania 13, 16, 26, 39, 94, 98, 112, 118, 123, 126, 127, 129
   Archaeological Museum 106

Arsenal 106, 107
Bastion of Schiavo-Lando 105
Chalepe Quarter 107
Chiones Quarter 107
Evraiki Quarter 106
Gulf of 105
Kastelli 90, 106, 117
Kastelli Quarter 105
Naval Museum 107
Plateia 1897 105
Plateia 1866 105
Renieri Gate 107
San Francesco, Church of 106
San Rocco, Church of 106, 107
San Salvatore, Church of 107
Splanzia Quarter 107
Tophanas Quarter 107
Charakas 90
chemists 130
Chora Sfakion 109, 110, 115
Chortatzia, Georgios 98
Chrissofakis, Spyros 87
cinemas 129, 130
climbing 127
Constantine, Emperor 24
Constantine, King 27
Constantinople 24, 25, 101
Corinth 22
Creta Beach Hotel 127
Creta Maris Hotel 50
Crete, Battle of 108, 109
Cronus 18
Crusades, the 25
Cyclades 13, 18, 19, 21
Cyprus 15, 21, 22, 106

D
Daliannis, Michalis 110, 111
Damaskinos, Mikhailis 41, 102
Damborgis, Ioannis 98
Darius 23
Delphi 22
dentists 130
Deucalion 20
Dia 49
Dictaean Cave 18, 64, 100, 128
Dikti mountains 13, 49, 64, 89
Diktyna 116, 117
doctors 130
Drosoulites 111
Drys 118

E
Ectabana 23
Egypt 20, 21, 33, 36, 46, 53
Eileithyia 50
Elgin Marbles 23
El Greco 39, 41, 102
El Greco Hotel 100
Elounda 56, 57, 58, 59, 126
  Beach Hotel 59, 60, 127
Episcopi 100
Episcopi Church 82
Etna, Mount 18
Euripides 23
Evans, Sir Arthur 19, 33, 34, 35, 36, 38, 45, 46, 52

F
fauna 129
Fira 125
fishing 126, 127
Flamininus 24
Fortezza 99
Fotakis, Efstratios 98
frescoes 26, 38, 46, 62, 101, 117, 118

G
galaktoboureko 121
Gaza 23
George, Prince 107, 108
Gortyn 17, 25, 92
Gournes 16, 50, 64, 90
Gournia 38, 44, 82, 92
Gramvousa 116, 118
Greece, National Tourist Organisation of 31

H
Hadrian 24
Halbherr, Federico 36, 91
Hassan Pasha, Mosque of 105
Heracles 17, 18
Heraklion 13, 19, 26, 33, 34, 48, 50, 51, 63, 64, 94, 102, 123, 125, 126, 127, 128
  Airport 14, 49
  Archaeological Museum 33, 34, 35, 36, 41, 42, 45, 46, 92
  Atlantis Hotel 41, 47
  Chania Gate 42
  Evans Street 42, 47
  Historical Museum, 45
  Kainouria Gate 42

Martinengo Bastion 42
Rocca al Marc fort 40
St George's Gate 42, 48
St Mark's Church 40
St Mina's Church 41
Venetian Armoury 40
Venetian Loggia 40
Homer 15, 17, 18, 50, 91
Hotel Alice, Sitia 83
hunting 127

I
icons 25, 26, 41, 45, 84, 100, 102, 123
Ideon Hotel 99
Idi Cave 100, 103
Idi Mountain 13, 49, 94, 95, 96
Ierapetra 15, 26, 86, 88, 89, 91, 127
    Hotel Alice, 87
Istanbul 40
Italy 21

J
Jason and the Argonauts 18

K
Kaiser, the 27
Kali Limenes 91
kalamarakia 121
Kalomenopoulos, Georgios 98
Kamares ware 37, 42, 44, 91
Kandanos 117, 118
Karpathos 83, 125
Kato Zakro 84
Katharo Plain 63
Kavalariana 118
Kavousi 83
Kazantzakis, Nicos 42
Keftia 21
Khrysolakkas 44, 52
Kissamos 117
Kissamou Gulf 117
Knossos 15, 17, 19, 20, 25, 33, 34, 35, 36, 37, 38, 42, 44, 45, 46, 51, 52, 90, 91, 104, 123
    Beach Hotel 50, 127
    Palace of 36
Kolimvari 117
Komitadhes 110
Kotsyfos, Gorge of 100
Kouneni 117
Kourtalioti, Gorge of 100
Koutsounari 88

Krakatoa 20
Kreipe, General Karl 95
Krita Hotel 87
Kritsa 61, 62, 63
Kydonia 107

L
Lappae 100
Lasithi, Plain of 50, 61, 63, 64
Lato 17, 58, 63, 117
Lavris Hotel 99
Lefka Ori 13, 108, 112
Levant, the 21
Levi, Professor Doro 91
Libya 23
Linear-A 37, 38, 44, 85, 93, 106
Linear-B 19, 35, 44, 92, 104
Lissos 107
lithinria (sea bream) 121
Lotus Eaters, The 16
Luce, Professor J.V. 21

M
Mackenzie, Duncan 35
madinatha 59
Malia 16, 37, 48, 51, 53, 64, 82
    Beach Hotel 51
    Gulf of 51
    Palace of 51, 52, 53
Maleme 108, 116, 117
    Beach Hotel 108
Maria, Grand Duchess 108
Masada 96
Matala 91, 93, 126
    Bay Hotel 91
meltemia 16, 49, 50, 51, 91
Messera 42
    Plain 91
Metaxas, Ioannis 27, 28
Meteora Monastery 102
Metellus Creticus 25
Milos 125
Minoa Hotel 83
Minoans, the 33, 44
    culture of 42, 50, 52, 57, 82, 84, 85, 90, 106, 125
    middle period 37, 92, 93
    late period 38, 57, 92, 93
Minos, King 19, 36
Minos Beach Hotel 59, 127
Minotaur, the 19, 36
Mirabello, Gulf of 55, 61, 63, 81, 126

136 *Index*

Mires 90, 91
Mokhlos 57, 82
Monastiraki 102
Morosini Fountain 40, 41, 47
Morosini, Francesco 40
Moss, Stanley 95
Mount Athos Monastery 101
Moussourosa, Markos 98
Moustafa, Pasha 110
Mussolini 27
Mycenaeans 38
Myriokefala 100
Myntos 57

N
Neapolis 50, 53, 64
newspapers 130
Nikephoros Phokas, Emperor 25
Nirou Chani 50

O
Ochi Day 28
Odysseus 18
Olympus, Mount 17, 22
Omalos, Plain of 113
ornithology 128
Ottoman Empire 26, 34

P
Palaikestro 38, 44
Paleochora 117
Paleokastrou 84
Palestine 21
Panaghia Kera, Church of 62, 81
Panzayios, Barba 59
Parthenon 23
Partisans, the 28
paximathi 121
Pefkos 89, 90
Perama 96
Persepolis 23
Persia 23
Petres 109
Petres River Beach 99
Phaistos 17, 19, 20, 36, 37, 38, 44, 51, 52, 90, 93
Phaistos Disc 44
Philistines 21
Pigi 90
Piraeus 39, 57, 123, 125
Pirgos 90

Plaka 59
Plakia 100
Platanos 117, 118
Plateia Eleutherias 41, 42, 47
Plato 21, 22, 23
Plaza Hotel 106
Pollyrrhenia 117, 118
Portugal 36
postage 131
Prevalakis, Michael 98
Prevelakis, Professor Pandelis 97
Preveli Monastery 100
Pseira 44, 57
Psychro 64

R
raki 59, 120
Ravenna 24
Rethymna Hotel 99
Rethymnon 13, 16, 26, 50, 94, 96, 97, 102, 108, 123, 126, 127, 129
   Archaeological Museum 99
   Arimondi Fountain 97
   Loggia 99
Rhea 18
   Hotel 56
Rhea, Temple of 92
Rhodes 21, 57, 83, 125
riding 127, 128
Rodopos 116, 117
Rousties 100
Roxana 24
Rubens 17

S
sailing 126
St Paul 24
   Chapel of 115
Samaria, Gorge of 15, 30, 50, 109, 112, 113, 114, 115, 128
Samos 27
Santorini 20, 21, 34, 37, 45, 82, 85, 125
Saracens, the 25, 39
Schliemann, Heinrich 18, 21, 34
scuba-diving 126
Second World War 27, 28, 40, 89, 99, 104, 117
Selenari, Gorge of 53
Sfakia 30, 82, 96, 109
Shakespeare 17
Sicily 21
Sirens Beach Hotel 51

Sitia 26, 57, 61, 82, 83, 127
　mountains 82
Skalani 47
skin-diving 126
Smyrna 27
Snake Goddess 44
snakes 129
Socrates 23
Sophocles 23
Souda 105
Souda Bay 108
Spain 36
Sparta 22
Spengler, Oswald 19
Spinalonga 26, 57, 58
Stalis 50, 51, 127
Suza 23
swimming 126, 127

T
tennis 127
Thavaras, Costas 57
Theotokopoulos, Domenico 102
Theseus 19, 36
Thessalonika 39
Thira 20
Tholos tombs 37
Thronos 102
Timbaki 89, 91
Toplou Monastery 83, 84
tourist police 31
Trojan War 17
Troy 18, 22, 23, 34
Tunis 86
Tunisia 21

Turkey 18
tyropitta 121

U
Uranus 18

V
Vai 15, 84, 85
Valaris Hotel 99
Vamos 108
vendetta 29
Venizelos, Eleutherios 26, 27, 108
Versailles Peace Conference 27
Vrakhasion 53
Vrondisi Monastery 102
Vryses 108

W
walking 127, 128
water-skiing 126, 127
weights and measures 131
White Mountains 13
Who Pays the Ferryman? 16, 58
windmills 51
Wunderlich, Professor Hans Georg 19, 20, 35

X
Xenia Hotel 100
Xerxes 23
Xyloskalon 113

Z
Zakro 38, 44, 57, 84, 85
Zakro, Palace of 84
Zeus 18, 64, 100